The Secret Letters of Jan van Riebeeck

The Secret Letters of Jan van Riebeeck

Translated and edited by
Robert Kirby

PENGUIN BOOKS

PENGUIN BOOKS
Published by the Penguin Group
27 Wrights Lane, London W8 5TZ, England
Viking Penguin, a division of Penguin Books USA Inc, 375 Hudson Street,
New York, New York, 10014, USA
Penguin Books Australia Ltd, Ringwood, Victoria, Australia
Penguin Books Canada Ltd, 10 Alcorn Avenue, Toronto, Ontario, Canada
M4V 3B2
Penguin Books (NZ) Ltd, 182-190 Wairau Road, Auckland 10, New Zealand
Penguin Books, Amethyst Street, Theta Ext 1, Johannesburg, South Africa

Penguin Books Ltd, Registered Offices: Harmondsworth, Middlesex,
England

First published by Penguin Books 1992
Copyright © Robert Kirby 1992

ISBN 0 140 17765 5

Designed and typeset by Jo Worthington-Smith DTP Design cc, Cape Town
Printed and bound by The Natal Witness
Cover designed by Hadaway Illustration & Design

For my great friend
Terry Stephan

Foreword

Shortly after he arrived at the Cape of Good Hope, Jan van Riebeeck continued a lively and revealing correspondence he'd been having with his second cousin, Hendrick Wessel van Lynhogg, a lay surgeon who lived near the town of Zjdehofdt in northern Holland. The flow of letters between the two had started some years before when van Riebeeck was still in Batavia. The letters were dispatched to and fro on boats of the Dutch East India Company, sometimes three or four arriving at the same time.

In 1676 van Lynhogg died, an unrehabilitated drug addict, and the letters were found bundled haphazardly in a cabin trunk in the attic of his house. Realising their importance as an historical record of happenings in the early Cape Colony, his wife tried to have them destroyed. However, van Lynhogg's surviving twin son managed to save some eighty per cent of them, handing them on to officials of the Dutch East India Company.

The letters were placed in the vaults of the Company and forgotten. Nearly two hundred years later they surfaced again, this time in the possession of one Heloise von Moelendorff, a retired Flemish gym-instructress living in Amsterdam. For a hefty price she sold them to South African interests.

Under the 340-Year-Rule the long secret letters of the Cape Colony's first Commander have now at last been released to public gaze. In this selection, kindly lent by the trustees of the South African van Riebeeck Letters Trust, a few of Jan van Riebeeck's letters to his cousin are published for the first time.

Editor's Note

In translating and editing the letters of Jan van Riebeeck my task has been both a delightful and a simple one: to select material of the greatest interest, not only to represent the true character of the writer, but to bring forward from history a fascinating glimpse of South Africa's parturition.

The task has been filled with joy. Quite often I felt as if I had travelled backwards in time, actually visited and spent weeks in that crude mud-and-daub fort with those earnest and stern men and women who built and peopled it. I felt I had been sitting at those rough tables and eating that simple food, attending the prayer meetings and the floggings and generally sharing the pioneer experience with them. Theirs must have seemed a sisyphean struggle as they patiently began to impose the cultures and habits of Europe onto their new and savage land.

So, along with the joy, my task was often disturbed by the uplifting realisation that the spirited Founding Fathers of the great country that South Africa has become often shared exactly the same doubts and fears that we, today, still experience. We have come a long way since 1652, and yet we have come no way at all.

In the translation there were a few problems. The language and phraseology of van Riebeeck's personal letters were not of the formal tone that marked his Day Book. Obviously his cousin, Hansie, was not only a relative but a close confidant, too; and so the letters were far more relaxed in tone and content. Here and there they refer clearly to such a condition of the relationship. In their early years the two men got drunk together, they got into bar brawls, visited brothels, they did all the other things that two healthy young males would have done in any society. It was only the fact of van Riebeeck's peripatetic career that split the friendship, leaving it to be conducted through the mail.

On all occasions I have tried to keep closely to van Riebeeck's rather unique style of writing. Often his Dutch was explicit, hence: *Djy plekka is runden uujt as inner warum pyjn in mjy ballen!* could only be rendered honestly as *this place has turned out to be a real ball-ache!* In the same way the line: *Aijl djy tydtt hyt hooler djy kek mousjadjell mit dijimm oegballer gekyjk* had to be realised as: *all the while eyeballing the keg of muskadel*, thereby preserving both the faintly slangy feel of the phrase and its placing in the present continuous tense.

This page, from a letter sent on 16th September 1656, is followed by my translation of it. Here van Riebeeck reflects on a lunch he had with a passing British captain who had brought along his own translator.

So, onst hyjt geklaaren myjt den soppje teo Flagstone hyjt beginq gegroyter myt datte hoorenlyjt Ingilse faabityj, djty eine vayjt sjy datt Kaapen Vijyn Gooejde Hoop eist waarum eine Ingelsej eijnerskappq.

"Myjen Kyjpttein seggen ditj det onner fuqt dkye Ingilse wassen hir in dem Kaapen ierjste, oudje vruugtjie," seg Kokkaas. "Hjy siggen datj Francis Drake wasetr heir verbyj innert 1580, langgert bjy verrin joelie Jaapens heir joeliens vingerts ujtgetrken hyt. Hjy onthouj datten eijrs in 1595 hyjt joelens jn paar vanner joelen bevokkeded buitens heir ge stuujq."

Well, we'd scarcely got through the soup when Flagstone started expanding on that hoary old Englishman's fable, the one that says that the Cape of Good Hope is, in fact, an English possession.

"My Captain says that of course the English were here in the Cape first, old fruit," said Smegma with a gratuitous smile. "He says that Francis Drake got here in 1580, long before you Dutchies got your act together. He recalls it was only in 1595 that you sent a couple of your rundown boats out here."

When it came to the use of terms like *Savage* and *Hottie* I felt that, as translator, it would be a more honest decision to use them in their original form and not try to change them to modern and fashionable Market Theatre-approved usages like *Natives* and *Cape Spanish*. Obviously their use is with the obvious rider that in those far-off days the words were not applied in any pejorative sense but in fact were rather kindly terms. The reader should be careful, therefore, to see them in context.

So it came to the selection of which letters to publish in this first edition. Here my task was at its most difficult. Jan van Riebeeck's letters are so full of surprise, humour and their expositions of the conflicting emotions of sorrow and joy. What collocation of these could possibly hope to transmit all this feeling across the years? There are something like four hundred letters, if one is to include the shorter ones. I have chosen twenty for this first edition.

Readers will note that the first one is dated June 1654, some two years after van Riebeeck had landed. It must be remembered that it took nearly two years for the Forte to be completed and that during the time of its construction van Riebeeck and his staff lived under canvas. Some letters from this period do exist but are rather short and disjointed. I chose to begin with letters written after van Riebeeck had moved in and had his own office.

The dates are, as far as possible, accurate. On some of the letters van Riebeeck either forgot to or simply didn't bother to add a date. Where this was the case, I have made extensive reference to the official journals and tried to place the letters with at least a vague chronological accuracy. In all cases where the date was not recorded I have added the "?" after the date stated.

I hope that the reader enjoys these letters as much as I did in translating them. The privilege was more than I deserve – to try to bring to our turbulent age a glimpse of the deep social and Christian compasssion that Commander Jan van Riebeeck held with such conviction and responsibility.

RK – Franschhoek 1992

The Forte de Goede Hoop
2nd June 1654

My Dear Hansie

Last week we finished stuffing our first Bushman. As I think I told you, I had asked the Commanding Officer of a small expeditionary force which was going up towards Namaqualand if he could bring me back a goodly specimen. And so he did. They got this fellow quite late one afternoon when they saw him stalking a Gemsbok. It was a lucky shot. The musket ball got him in the back of the thigh which brought him down. The lads were then able to dispatch him with a few sharp blows to the skull and without any further damage to the skin. They packed him in salt and got him here in mint condition.

Luckily, Cheese Blaauwtjopp had taken a few lessons in taxidermy when he was studying at the Leiden Colonial Institute, and was dying to get his hand in again. I gave him the body and told him to get on with it.

Well, our little Bushie is opposite me as I write this. Cheese has made a beautiful job of him. He mounted him, standing on a small rock in a typical attitude, little bow and arrow poised and the sweetest expression on his wizened little yellow face as he peers at his prey. A few of his primitive artefacts are scattered around his feet. I think Cheese overdid the buttocks a bit, but by and large the effect is startlingly lifelike.

What we're going to do is set up a little museum to offer some instruction to the officers and crews of passing ships, give them an idea of what the interior of this country is like. So I've asked the Commanding Officer to try and get a couple more, specifically a nursing female and a couple of dusty children so that we can have a proper Bushman family group.

And Cheese has come up with a very good idea. He says that we could get something quite profitable going. There are hundreds of other tribes out here. Every hill you cross there's a new one. Surely someone in Europe wants a record of all this and will pay good money for well-stuffed specimens. So, if you get a chance next time you're in Amsterdam, ask around a few of the museums for me.

Otherwise, I can't tell you what a ball-ache this place has turned out to be. Yesterday I had to receive and then sit and listen patiently to a deputation from the local Khoi-Khoi Civil Rights Association. It was one long bitter complaint, and believe me, these people know how to complain. Apparently over weekends a few of my fellows have been going to the Hottie settlements getting drunk on potent Hottie liquor and, in their need for a little extra merriment, have been bringing the Hottie women back to the Forte and taking them into their beds. Surprise, surprise.

As you know, I long ago put a severe ban on this. We can't have these frightful women shrieking around the corridors at all hours of the night. You have no idea how these creatures like to steal. A lot of the administrative staff are missing God only knows what.

Something had to be done so I called the lads together in the courtyard and gave them a talking to.

"Look," I said. "We know that we're all a long way away from our homes and families and wives and, in many cases, brothels. But that doesn't mean we have to start behaving in an irresponsible fashion."

There were a few mutters at that. "Now, look. I don't see any major harm arising if a few of you get together in a small gang or two and go and waylay a few of the Hottie womenfolk as they trudge back from their root-gathering expeditions. Have a bit of fun is what I say. But leave it at that."

That raised a desultory cheer from one or two of the clerks. I went on, trying to keep a serious tone in my voice.

"What I don't want to see is you bringing these women back here to the Forte. You know what they're like. With the best of intentions you try to show them a bit of what civilised life can be like, and before you can say Dutch East India Company they've sneaked off to the kitchen, helped themselves to our victuals and scuttled back into the hills."

There was a general mumble at this. I decided to change the emphasis. "What I'm saying is that we have to be careful with these people," I insisted. "The Hottentot is a strange fellow and has strange ways of thinking. If we start playing around with his women too much we will get right up his nose and he will refuse to continue helping us with the new jetty and then where will we be?"

Well, they seemed to have got the message. They muttered a bit more and went about their business. I don't think this is going to be the end of the problem, though. The K-KCRA spokesman said that one or two of his women were now pregnant and that he's going to be demanding compensation if the progeny look even slightly light-skinned.

By the way, talking about brothels. A fellow off one of the east-bound ships told me that he'd been up in the Hook, offloading some spices, and he'd seen you at Madam Zzaj's place, Haarlem Moon, last September. Now there are some fond memories! If you get around there again please give my best to Penelope Rott. She's the big strawberry blonde with the harelip.

My best to Hendrina and the little ones.

Yours in God

Van

**The Forte de Goede Hoop
26th October 1654**

Dear Old Hansie

The vexed question of a new language has again raised its head. I think I told you that this idea has been punted around for over two years now by Cheese Blaauwtjopp. In fact he first proposed the idea on board the *Drommedaris* coming out here.

We'd just flung a couple of new scurvy casualties overboard and were getting down to a pleasant game of deck quoits, when he dumped this one on us.

"Look," he said, "we're going to a brand new country. We'll be the first white men to settle there. Why don't we make up a new language?"

"What's suddenly the matter with the one we've got?" I asked.

He was ready for that one. "It's going to be far too complicated to teach to all the Savages," he said. "They are simple people, Jannie. They need a simple language."

At the time it seemed like a good idea. But the subject wasn't raised seriously for some time. We had so much to do getting settled in and getting the garden under way, not to mention building the Forte. Cheese brought up his idea now and then, but it wasn't until at breakfast last Tuesday that he raised it again in earnest.

"I've been thinking about the new language," he said suddenly.

I got in as quick as a flash. "It's a wonderful idea, Cheese," I said. "I'm going to put it down in the Journal. But I have to tell you that I don't think we're going to have the time. Making up a brand new language isn't as easy as it sounds."

He had an answer ready. "We aren't going to have to make up a completely new one," he said with that nasty little smug grin on his face. "What we are going to do is take our own language and adapt it."

"Adapt it?" I said doubtfully.

"What we do is we take Dutch and we cut out all the grammar. You know, the difficult participles and prepositions, tenses, all that stuff."

I couldn't believe my ears. "What?"

"And we'll have the basis of a whole new language," he finished triumphantly. "We can add a few Savage and Hottie words here and there, you know, to give it a little colour. And then we can claim we made it up all on our own."

I put down my teacup. "Now listen, Cheese," I said slowly. "You can't take a perfectly serviceable language like Dutch and start to mess around with it. The Lords Seventeen will have a fit."

He opened his mouth but I pressed on. "What is more," I added sternly, "I have recently been having a peep at some of the local Savage languages. And they are very complicated languages, too."

"So?"

"So, we can't have the heathen hordes pouring in here and finding us talking a language that hasn't got any grammar. I can just see it. Some Savage chief pitches up here in his tribal skins, stands in front of us and says in his own language something like: 'The pleasure of your estimable and gracious company and presence in our land is something which has long been denied us and we foresee copious benefit arising from a sensible, affable and mutually acceptable collocation of our collective and individual needs and talents.'

"What's he going to think when the white man answers: 'No fine. I is please you have visited by us. No, us seek no more of your wives no.'?"

I could see Cheese wasn't going to be put off easily. "The trouble with you," he said sourly, "is that you're scared of progress."

"It's not progress I'm scared of," I said. "It's making us look like a bunch of ill-educated pricks."

"We have to communicate," he said petulantly.

"So let's learn one of their languages," I said.

"Are you crazy?" he said. "The Savage's languages are far too difficult. There was an article in the *Market Gardener's Weekly*. They were talking about one of the Savage languages up north – something called Tsoeloe. They said that it could take as much as five years to learn just the basic verbs."

"The *Market Gardener's Weekly* is a Portuguese magazine," I said quickly. "You can never rely on those."

The argument would have gone on, but our tame Hottentot, Harry, ran in just then. Apparently some of his bloody feral brethren had been raiding our broccoli garden again. He says they think that broccoli has some sort of magic properties. It just makes me fart.

And now the bad news. Maria is definitely on her way back from her shopping holiday in Europe. I know because the

Vuildirk sailed in here last week and delivered an advance load of her luggage. Fourteen sea-trunks full of petticoats! I've got quite used to not having her around and I don't know how I'm going to cope having my serene bachelor existence ruptured. I've taken some precautions, though. I got together a small working group and we went exploring for somewhere I could build a little shack, a private hidey-hole I'll be able to run to when things get domestically hot. We combed the surrounding area and eventually found a pleasant wooded slope not two miles from the Forte, with a beautiful little clearing and a bubbling crystal stream running through it. I've decided to call it Bellville.

More of that later. Hottentot Harry just ran in again and says that they've caught one of the broccoli thieves. I must be off to supervise the flogging.

Love to Hendrina and the kids.

Yours in God

Van

My Dear Hansie

It's two o'clock in the morning as I sit writing this. Half an hour ago I woke from the most dreadful nightmare. It was quite awful and I couldn't get back to sleep. I decided that instead of lying there listening to Maria snoring I'd get this down to you while it was still fresh in my mind.

The damned English were here again this week. If there is one prediction I can make with certainty, it is this. If ever any Englishmen get involved in developing or running this country you can be sure that they'll screw it up. I have never come across a nation of people so solemnly dedicated to hypocrisy, to lies, perjury and deceit.

In this case a ship called *The Greyhound* hove into the bay. Duly its snot-gobbling captain, one Jeremiah Flagstone, presented himself at the Forte, bringing with him a couple of his poofy officers. I've told you how Cheese Blaauwtjopp loathes the Portuguese, but at least he's prepared to pass the time of day with them. When it comes to the English he refuses point blank to have anything to do with them until such time as they start taking regular baths. When he saw their ship at anchor, his first suggestion was that we quietly murder the lot of them, sail their vessel into deep water and sink it. Of course I couldn't agree, so he slunk off to his quarters and a four-day sulk leaving me to deal with them on my own.

Well, having put up with these people I now think that Cheese's idea had a lot of merit. I have never seen such bombast.

Flagstone and his mates ponced around the Forte sticking their long English noses into all the corners, asking questions and passing scurrilous opinions on how we were doing things. They criticised the way we were handling the Savages and the Hotties. They had a lot to say about the construction of the Forte, implying that it would be a lot safer if English designs had been used.

They refused to speak Dutch, calling it a vulgar language and implying that the world's civilised people only speak English. Instead they brought along what they called their interpreter, a particularly grimy Hottentot called Smegma, whom they'd picked up years before somewhere on the north coast.

I tolerated all this, deciding that I'd return their rudeness with an example of Dutch diplomacy at its best. What changed my mind was yesterday when I had Flagstone to a farewell lunch. Maria kicked up a hell of a fuss about the interpreter, saying that she wasn't prepared to sit at the same table as a Hottie.

"He can speak English," I explained.

"That makes it even worse," she replied.

I calmed her down and said it would only be for an hour and that none of the local Hotties would get to hear about it so that was no problem.

Well, we'd scarcely got through the soup when Flagstone started expanding on that hoary old Englishman's fable, the one that says that the Cape of Good Hope is in fact an English possession.

"My Captain says that of course the English were here in the Cape first, old fruit," said Smegma with a gratuitous smile. "He says that Francis Drake got here in 1580, long before you

Dutchies got your act together. He recalls it was only in 1595 that you sent a couple of your rundown boats out here."

"Tell your Captain that might be so, but the Portuguese got here a long time before Drake," I retorted sweetly. "A small matter of ninety-two years before. In case your Captain hadn't heard, a fellow called Batholomew Diaz sailed past here in that year. And then nine years later another one called Vasco da Gama actually stopped here. If anyone's got prior claim to this place, it's the da Porroes."

While Smegma translated this, Maria leaned over and hissed in my ear.

"Van, tell the Hottie to use a spoon and please not drink straight out of the plate."

Smegma translated Flagstone's answer. "My Captain says that of course we only have Diaz's and da Gama's words on that," said Smegma. "After all, they were Portuguese. In his opinion this place rightfully belongs to the English as they were here before the Dutch," he added with a sniff.

"Then ask your Captain why the English didn't settle here while they had the chance?" I retorted cleverly. He gabbled away while Maria glared at him. Flagstone's answer was outrageous.

"My Captain says that the English could quite easily have colonised the Cape of Good Hope in 1580, but they decided they'd allow the Dutch to settle here first."

"That was so nice of them," I remarked with a grim smirk.

"My Captain says there were very good reasons for this decision. He says the English acknowledge that the Dutch are very good at starting off settlements in primitive lands, at doing all the rough work like bush-clearing and planting vegetables and fruit trees and killing off the more dangerous inhabitants."

Maria kicked me under the table. "Van, tell the Hottie he's eating tomato bredie and please he mustn't use his fingers," she muttered.

Smegma continued smoothly. "My Captain says the English are quite happy to let the Dutch stay here for the meantime and get on with it. He says his orders are to have a look around the place and take back a report to the House of Lords."

Maria kicked me again. "Van, tell the Hottie he must please not wipe his mouth dry with the back of his arm. He must use a slice of bread like we do."

Smegma went on. "He says there is no doubt that the House of Lords will write a letter to you telling you what else they want done. Then, as soon as they are satisfied that the Dutchies have done a proper job in developing this place, the House of Lords will then decide when the English will come back and take you over."

That was a bit too much to stomach. "Tell your Captain to listen carefully," I said grimly. "Tell him we've heard these threats before from the Portuguese and from other passing Limies like your Captain. Tell him I want him to know that so long as there's even one solitary Dutchman here, sitting on his stoep sucking at his pipe and farting into his cushion, no Englishmen will ever take it over. We'd die first."

On having this repeated to him, Flagstone smirked. Smegma translated his answer. "My Captain says you mustn't take on so, dear boy," he said. "The English have no intention of arriving here and taking you by force. Instead they will use the most

ating of all weapons the Englishman possesses. They will
over the way they are presently taking over most of the
a mixture of spite, bullshit and low cunning."

as finished in a slightly strained atmosphere. I
with them to their longboat.

ke as they were getting into it. "My Captain says
ing in quite a good report on you, but in the
ests that you do something about improving
tisfactory Forte you have built. He says that
us...   ch makes it look like it was designed by
nignogs. The English would like you to get going on a better one
built of stones."

"My Captain says he'll see you in a year or two," shouted
Smegma as they rowed off.

"Tell your Captain to go and piss up his mainsail," I shouted
back, and gave them the old one-finger salute. I stalked back to
the Forte. Cheese was waiting for me, a malicious grin all over
his face.

"What did I tell you about the English?"

I waved him away. "The last thing I want to think about or talk
about right now is drip-nosed Englishmen."

"I bet you they told you they were going to come back here
and take over," he went on.

"How did you know?"

"Because the Pommies are always doing that," he said. "And
the trouble is that people take them seriously. As a result a lot of
sleep is lost for nothing."

"They sounded quite serious to me."

He laughed softly. "Commander, you have to understand something about the English. They are natural liars. It's something that's bred into them. They'll lie about anything they see, they can't help it. And there are other reasons they'll never take over this country."

"What are they?"

"The Savages and the Hotties. The Englishman is a snob. He's quite incapable of dealing with primitives. He's just not capable of sinking down to their squalid barbarian level the way we Dutchmen are."

I didn't like that too much. Whatsmore I think he's wrong. The English will come back, they always do. Cheese would have none of it.

"This country could turn out to have great deposits of diamonds and gold and any other precious mineral you might think of. And we already know that it's got a cheap and available labour force that can be put to doing all the back-breaking labour necessary to get all this stuff out of the ground. The Englishman will consider it beneath him to have any part of it. You mark my words."

Maria was in a real snit all day and we went to bed on bad terms. And an hour ago I had the awful nightmare. In it the English had come back to the Cape and had, indeed, taken it over. And they hadn't used guile and deception either, just plain brute force. All the Dutchmen had been turned into slaves, forced to swear allegiance to the English throne. Worse than that, we had to start learning to speak English. We were all sent out into the fields and made to work. Hotties and Savages were put in charge of us.

In the dream I was in court, up on trial on a charge of trying to steal The Cape of Good Hope. I said that was a lie. But this great fat English judge told some Hottentot soldiers to torture me. I was dragged off to the rack and strapped down. As they started turning the wheel I began screaming. I woke up in a cold sweat.

To end on a happier note. A few of the local Hottentots have formed a dance band. They got hold of some squashboxes and lutes and drums and they're not bad at all, whipping up polkas and gavottes and the occasional waltz. They call themselves The Hottie Seven and I can tell you, these long summer nights have become a lot more fun.

Give my best to Hendrina and if you see a passing Englishman kick him in the teeth for me.

Yours in God

Van

**The Forte de Goede Hoop
May 1655 (?)**

My Dear Hansie

Do you remember those wonderful words in Job? The ones that went: 'They were driven forth from among men to dwell in the cliffs and in the rocks. Among the bushes they brayed, under the nettles they were gathered together. They were children of fools, yea, children of base men : they were viler than the earth.'

I've always wondered why Job wasn't more specific. From the description I've always assumed he was talking about the English or the Portuguese. But I've changed my mind now that we've discovered a brand new sub-species of the Hottentots. If you ask me I'd far rather they had never been discovered. They really are an objectionable lot. Sometimes the ways of the Lord puzzle me.

I think I told you in a previous letter about what we call the Strandlopers, indigent riffraff who are too lazy to work for a living, preferring to exist off the crabs and dead fish they can scavenge on the beaches. Well, Nerina Grobb, the do-gooder wife of our resident blacksmith, has been doing some charity work amongst these pitiful creatures, trying – not very successfully, I might add – to instil some sort of Protestant work ethic in them. She'd picked up a few words of their rudimentary tongue. Listening to their silly chatter she realised that there was something worth investigating.

She asked some questions and they reluctantly directed her to the slopes of Table Mountain. Lo and behold! There they were, a few hundred of them living in caves and rude shelters.

We've called these ones Berglopers, and a strange lot they are, too. They're twice as lazy as the Strandlopers but they steal three times as much. Nerina says she was only there for twenty minutes but they managed to filch her handbag, her wristwatch, one shoe and her bra. They then started calling her a 'rubbish' and chased her down the mountain.

Despite this she was terribly excited and said she wanted to do some further study on them. I told her to forget it.

"We've got enough problems down here without having even more indolent barbarians swarming all over the place," I said firmly.

But you know how insistent women can be. To shut her up I agreed to go and have a look for myself. My sense of blind trust doesn't spread quite as far as Nerina's, so I took a dozen of the lads with me.

It's easy to find the place. You climb up to the neck at the end of Table Mountain and take the game path south. This soon peters out, but then all you have to do is follow the empty bottles. It took us an hour to reach their village, tucked away in amongst the buttresses. You have never seen such squalor. And if you think their shelters are rude you should hear their language.

We tried to communicate with them. Their spokesperson came leaping out, some ghastly raddled crone with no teeth and a halitosis that would have embarrassed a walrus. She was clothed in what appeared to be some old flour sacks and which looked rather familiar. That and the fact that she spoke a sort of kindergarten Dutch made me realise that she must have been spending some time lurking around the Forte.

In between all her obscenities I gathered that all she wanted to know was whether we'd brought any liquor with us. I told her that she'd better stop swearing.

"You mustn't think you are dealing with just some of your ungodly associates," I told her. "We are refined and gentle people. We are Christians."

She took no notice, so I told four of the lads to give her a couple of swift kicks and bashes around the head with their musket butts. After that she calmed down a bit and we managed to get some sense out of her.

The problem seems to be that these Berglopers – as they are called – are not at all popular with their cousins, the more common Flatland Hottentots. Whatsmore, they don't tame as easily as the Flatties do and so they can't be used for casual labour around the vegetable gardens. Which is probably a good thing given their more highly developed thieving skills.

Still, I'm not prepared to ignore their plight and so I've arranged to have some food parcels sent up there on a regular basis. I told Cheese Blaauwtjopp to tell Nerina Grobb she was strictly forbidden to go anywhere near them again. It was an instruction she didn't receive with any noticeable enthusiasm. She stormed into my office with her eyes blazing hotly.

"What do you mean I can't continue my studies of the Bergies?" she demanded.

"Exactly what I say, Nerina," I explained patiently. "We simply can't afford to get too friendly with these creatures."

"Why not?"

"Because it will lead to other things."

"Such as?"

I didn't quite know the answer to that, so I tried using reason – a mistake as it turned out.

"Nerina, I think what you are trying to do with the indigenes is most commendable. I'm sure there will be a lovely place for you in Heaven when you die." I put a lot of sing-song into my voice so she would know I was being sincere. "But you have to understand that there are limits. If you go on like this no one knows where it will all end up. The word will get around that we are an easy touch and we'll find ourselves saturated with Hotties of one kind or another trying to get something for nothing."

Her little white face was wreathed in concern. "They need our help," she cried.

"They've managed quite well for hundreds of years without our help," I said placatingly. "If we start just giving them every-thing they will suddenly find they have lost all their ability to look after themselves. And then where will they be?"

She turned on the taps then, started weeping and snivelling. I've heard about these sort of women in some of the other colo-nies and settlements. After a year or two away from their homes in Europe they start to develop these strange needs to be socially meaningful. Instead of staying at home and getting on with the sensible basic duties that women were put on this earth to do, they rush around the place looking for some or other unfor-tunates they can save. They're far worse than the missionaries.

"But I want to write important international novels about their tragic suffering, misery and pain," she howled. "There was a woman in Formosa who wrote books about the anguish and afflictions amongst the Malays. She got an important inter-national book prize for them."

"We're not here to get important international book prizes," I explained. "We are here to grow vegetables."

She sniffed loudly.

"Now most of these vegetables are for the passing ships," I went on smoothly. "But some of them we keep for ourselves. Your job is to cook these vegetables for your husband. Does that make it clear?"

I could see that the wisdom of what I was saying had got through to her. She nodded through her tears.

When he heard about the Berglopers, Cheese Blauwtjopp said that the experience has shown us that what we really need to do here is get the matter of the numerous different racial types in this country onto a solid and preferably scientific basis. In this way it might stop people like Nerina going all soppy whenever they find a new one.

He said it was high time that we tried to draw up some sort of Tribes Register so that we know for sure in future who is who. He said we could have separate sections like Flatland Hottentots and Bergloper Hottentots and Strandloper Hottentots and Mountain Savages and Peaceful Savages and Dangerous Savages and Still To Be Discovered Savages and so on.

"This way," he said, "we'll be able to work out exactly how to treat each separate group and, more especially, how to keep them apart. And if anyone ever tries to cross from one group to the other we can bestow a really meaningful punishment on them like a stiff-rod beating or a drawn-out keelhaul."

"Do you think keeping people apart is a good idea?" I asked cautiously.

"It's good colonial management policy," he reassured me. "It allows each tribe to develop along its own cultural path. It allows us to designate where each tribe is going to live. It stops tribes from fighting with each other. And, best of all, it ensures racial purity so that we Dutch may continue to reproduce ourselves in the way that The Almighty intended us to be."

"It sounds wonderful," I breathed.

"It is wonderful, Commander. Dominee Graham Verwoerd was telling me the other day how well it worked when he was in Sumatra. Apparently some of the primitive forest-dwelling Savages started trying to claim back vast areas of the forest which had been theirs since antiquity and which the Dutch had expropriated for themselves."

"In the name of the Lord," I added quickly.

"Dominee Verwoerd said the Sumatran Governor at the time, The Esteemed Lord Snylshitt of Rotterdam, explained to the forest-dwellers that he'd set aside a whole twelve-morgen corner of the forest especially for them and he gave his word that the mighty armed force of the Dutch would guarantee that that corner of the forest would be theirs forever.

"Then he gave them some red beads and sent them happily on their way," he finished.

I think we might just have discovered the answer to all the problems of this weird country. I've told Cheese to get on with the Tribes Register, a task he's taken to with much enthusiasm. He's a wonderful Dutchman, our Cheese is. Whenever there's an obstacle to our journey along the virtuous paths of The Almighty, he always makes a plan.

Tell Hennie and the brats hullo from me.

Yours in God

Van

**The Forte de Goede Hoop
1st October 1655**

My Dear Hansie

I'm enclosing some interesting seeds. We had some visiting Savages here a couple of months ago and Hendryk Boom, our Chief Gardener, cadged a few from their witchdoctor. Apparently what they do is grow these big greenish weeds from the seeds and then they dry the leaves and smoke them. Hendryk says they insisted he shared a pipe with them. He said it was a very weird effect. First it just made him laugh a lot. Then, for a while he found he was actually enjoying the Savage's company. But then he vomited. Anyway, the witchdoctor swore by the stuff and said it just takes a little getting used to.

I told Hendryk to plant a little patch up behind the brinjals where they'll get enough sun. They've done very well, all about two feet high and with plenty of heads which Hendryk says he's found are the best bits to smoke. He's quite hooked on the stuff, you never see him that he isn't stuffing more into his pipe. I have to admit it's turned him into a far nicer sort of person. He's not nearly the surly little shit he used to be. I'm plucking up courage to try some myself. We've had a go at making wine here and I can tell you it's been a major disaster. It's obviously something to do with the soil. If they ever get a decent grape to grow in this God-forsaken place I'll be damned surprised. Anyway enough of that. Plant these and tell me what you think.

We had our first Coon Carnival last week. It's an idea cooked up by the local Hotties, a little concert they put together as a way of showing their gratitude to the white men for all we've sacrificed for them. They put a lot of effort into getting it right, months of preparation. One or two of their women have been working as sweepers in the uniform shop. Over the months they begged, borrowed and no doubt stole lots of cloth offcuts, buttons and thread and secretly made these amazing traditional Hottie costumes.

It turned out be quite a lot of fun. At about eleven-thirty last Saturday morning they came streaming out of their hovels and paraded around the Forte. They'd strung their traditional drums around their necks and one or two had fashioned primitive banjoes. We noticed with some interest that Gary Beneke's long lost bugle made its first public appearance since its theft last August.

It all went on about two hours. There was a lot of singing and dancing and I'd agreed to let some of the Madagascar slaves join in. I only wish they'd show that much energy when they work in the fields!

I've heard a lot about the famous natural sense of rhythm that primitive people are supposed to have, but I can't say I detected much of that. Except in a crude way they didn't sound too musical to me. Anyway, it was quite a fun morning and at the end of it one of the Hotties made a touching little speech about how much they had learned from white people and how they looked forward to better Hottentot-Dutch relationships in the future. At the end of the day they aren't such a bad crowd after all. Rounding off the proceedings with a hanging might have been a little insensitive of us, but at least Gary's got his bugle back.

Sorry this letter is bitty. Things have been very busy here with every new day bringing a new crisis and a new decision to be made. I've had to reduce the legal limit on crawfish again. It's that damned Loop Zennerwoudt and his family. They've been bringing in these tiny ten-pounders and there's nothing I can do to stop them. Apparently Zennerwoudt goes out in one of the longboats with that ghastly wife of his and all their ghastly children and brings back hundreds of the unfortunate things which he then sells to the Hotties. He says they aren't clever enough to catch them for themselves, which is a good thing, I suppose.

Anyway, I put up a notice saying this was absolutely the last time I was reducing the limit and that from now on out if anyone is caught with a crawfish under twelve pounds, I will personally see to his spending at least six months in the dungeons. Of course, Cheese Blaauwtjopp was full of advice on the matter. He says that by continually reducing the limit I am setting a very bad example for the future and that they'll just go on reducing it until all the crawfish are gone. I don't think so.

Some Scottish missionaries arrived here a fortnight ago. What a crowd of killjoys! I gave them the usual advice I give to opposition churchmen. "When you venture into the uncharted wilderness up there," I said, "whatever you do don't take guns. Your Bibles will give you all the protection you need against the murderous pagan hordes."

It hasn't failed yet. The last expedition has been gone eighteen months and we haven't heard a word.

All for now. Congratulations on the twins and love to Hennie.

Yours in God

Van

Forte de Goede Hoop
February 1656 (?)

Dear Old Hansie

How do you turn a Hottie into more of a shady, conniving thief than he is? How do you turn a Savage into more of an unGodly, treacherous villain than he already is? I'll tell you. You send him to a Dutchman for further instruction.

I've never been able to understand why we Dutch have this need to rip everyone off. Everywhere you go in the world today, there are Dutchmen with their fingers in the till up to the armpits. In Batavia it was just the same. We were bleeding the country dry. Why do we do it? I know the Spanish do their fair share of exploiting, but at least they are embarrassed about it. I know the English do it, but at least they cover up. But not the Dutchman. He just goes in and grabs whatever isn't nailed down. And when that isn't enough, he starts stealing from himself. We're getting as bad as the Portuguese.

You'll be wondering what brought all this to a head. Well, it all started when I began making enquiries about the sudden unexplained disappearance of about half the Forte's supply of rum. As you may know, each six months Head Office sends us out a regular supply of fifty barrels so that there's always some on hand for passing ships. We are not supposed to drink it ourselves.

I know that the occasional barrel gets quietly purloined for use in the barracks, and the officers' mess usually requisitions another two or three. I can live with that sort of shrinkage. What

I can't live with is the fact that no one here can explain to me why some twenty-eight other barrels have gone missing. I went down to the stores and demanded to know where they were. That underhand little bugger, Bagel Slyggtflugge was being as devious as he could.

"I don't know where they've gone, Commander," he whined. "It must have been the Hotties."

"You can't blame everything on the Hotties," I said angrily.

He was as quick as a flash. "Then it must have been the Savages," he retorted.

"Well, if either the Hotties or the Savages got in here and stole a couple of dozen large barrels of rum from under your nose, it doesn't say much for the security around here."

"That's not my fault, Commander," he said prissily. "I'm not in charge of security. You must go and talk to Sergeant Fanus Glom about that. That's his department."

They all do it. The moment anyone points a finger, the person at the other end of the finger immediately starts pointing his own finger at someone else. I called Cheese Blaauwtjopp into the office and told him to start making some serious enquiries. He didn't seem all that keen.

"Are you quite sure you want to pursue this matter, Commander?"

"Of course I want to pursue it," I answered angrily. "Some disgusting swine is ripping off our rum supplies. Whatsmore, when I find out who it is, the culprit will find himself on the business end of a couple of hundred lashes."

"I see," he said slowly.

"And while you're about it, I want you to have a quick look around some of the other departments. A little unannounced stocktaking. If someone's stealing rum, you can be damn sure some other sod is filching something else as well."

"Very well, Commander," he said. "But don't say I didn't warn you."

I didn't know what he was talking about. But I found out soon enough. I wish I could tell you that it was only rum that was disappearing. Three days later Cheese flounces into my office and slaps a great list on my desk.

"What's this?" I asked.

"It's only what you asked for, Commander. An up-to-date list of what's gone missing from the Forte supplies."

I looked at the list. I couldn't believe my eyes. A hundred and fifty sacks of flour, two leagues of uniform cloth, a year's supply of leather, dozens of barrels of nails, tar, screws, lantern oil, seeds, ointments, building materials. You name it, it's gone missing.

"I'm sorry the list is so short. I've only had three days," said Cheese.

"Are you trying to tell me that all this stuff has simply vanished?"

"So it would appear, Commander."

"Where?"

I sat with my mouth hanging open while he explained. It seems that certain of my staff have been doing a little private bartering with the Hotties and the Savages. It all started a couple of years ago when an exploratory group under that eminent swindler, Corporal Jacques Saggen, went up north. They met up with some friendly Griquas who took a shine to the boots the soldiers were wearing. Griquas had never even thought about boots, preferring to run around the countryside on the bare feet they were born with. They asked for a couple of pairs, offering something called powdered rhino horn in exchange. They offered to throw in a couple of their womenfolk but the soldiers, knowing how I feel about that sort of thing, said the rhino horn would be enough.

"What's so special about powdered rhino horn?" I asked Cheese.

"I'm afraid I can't answer that, Commander," he said with that look that told me he was lying in his teeth.

"And all the rest of this?" I asked, tapping the list.

"Well, one thing led to another. The word got around and other Savages and Hotties started arriving here with all sorts of other primitive goodies like ivory, crocodile skins, leopard pelts, ostrich feathers, secret Bushman sex aids. These things are very valuable back in Europe, Commander."

"In Europe?"

"Well, there are some sailors involved, too. They get a small cut for handling the transport."

It was clear that I would have to take some action.

"A couple of hundred lashes isn't going to be nearly enough, Cheese," I said pleasantly. "I am now appointing you as the head of an independent body of enquiry and by the end of next week you are going to supply me with a full report, including names."

"Is this absolutely necessary, Commander?"

"And tell the carpentry shop to get to work on a new set of gallows, one that can take at least four thieves at a time."

"I really believe you should think again, Commander."

"I've got nothing to think about, Cheese. I am not prepared to go down in history as the man who was in charge of a criminal colony. I have my name to think of."

"Of course, Commander," he said with a smirk. "And I must say that I think the action you are proposing is very commendable. This whole disgraceful matter needs to be brought out into the open so that your name gets cleared."

"Thank you, Cheese. I knew you'd see it my way."

"I see the *Vuildirk* is in harbour again," he continued. "She's sailing for the mother country tomorrow afternoon. I suggest that we get hold of the Captain and ask him to take this list back to Head Office."

"What?" I didn't like that too much.

He went on smoothly. "But you should also write a letter to go with it, Commander. So that your name is kept in the clear."

That didn't sound like a bad idea. I told him I'd think about it. When he'd left the office I had a closer look at his list. Half an hour later I called him back in.

"I've had a long think about all this," I began. "And I think that we should deal with this matter on our own."

"Oh?"

"I don't think there's any need to go worrying Head Office with what is really just a minor local matter."

"What has changed your mind, Commander?"

"Let's call it mature reflection. It's put a completely different complexion on the matter."

He narrowed his eyes. "I thought that a careful look at that list might change your mind, Commander," he said quietly.

We both knew what he was referring to. The damned rum. At least ten of the missing barrels had been delivered up here to my own quarters. Maria had signed for them. Of course, she uses the stuff strictly for medicinal purposes. She's not a strong woman and it helps her keep the dreaded flux at bay. But I knew it was useless to try to explain that to Cheese.

I looked him straight in the eye. "After going through your list there's no doubt in my mind that it must have been the Hotties and Savages who stole all the missing goods."

"And the rum," he added, unnecessarily.

"So what we need to do is make an example," I went on. "Get hold of Fanus Glom and tell him to nip out and capture a couple of really grubby Hotties. Tomorrow morning we'll have a quick public flogging. You can ask the Captain of the *Vuildirk* to come and watch."

"Why not use slaves, Commander?"

"Why slaves?"

"Then we can hang them as well. That'll go down a treat at Head Office."

"Excellent idea."

I should never have chosen Cheese to investigate the thing. He's far too devious and I'm sure he was covering up for himself, too.

I won't be writing for a couple of weeks. I'm going into the interior to check out the Savages.

Give Hendrina and the little ones a hug from me.

Yours in God

Van

My Dear Hansie

I think I wrote to you last year about the Berglopers, a particularly abominable strain of the Hotties who inhabit the cracks and caves up on the mountainside. And they've started to be a real problem, getting more brazen and wily in their raids on the Forte. Quite a few of their number have moved off the mountain and have set up shop in the bush quite near to the Forte and, therefore, their main source of supply.

The only natural gift the Almighty seems to have given these creatures is a profound cunning, and they use it with the experience of years. We don't even see them as they slide in and out of the Forte on their forays. They have taken petty theft to new heights.

In particular they like to steal anything that even looks like liquor. I've ordered extra guards and locks on the wine and rum supplies, but somehow they always seem to get to them. Not that they aren't receiving more than a little assistance from some of their Hottie cousins working for us in the Forte, creatures which we were Christian enough to lift out of their idle, peaceful aborigine lives and introduce to the industrious ways of the Lord.

I spoke to Sergeant Joggemaas Venker, our head of security. He's not the brightest of fellows but on this occasion he came up with a brilliant idea.

"What we must do, Commander, is set a trap for them," he said.

"A trap?" I said doubtfully.

"Once we've caught a couple of them, we'll make a public example of them. That'll do wonders."

"What sort of trap?"

He'd worked it all out, bless him. The following day we sent a small platoon of soldiers into the bush to roust the Bergies from their crude dwellings so that they wouldn't see what we were up to. With this diversion underway, we set a couple of our less indolent slaves to work, digging a deep pit in a clearing south of the Forte.

It took nearly all the day and late that afternoon we made final arrangements. We covered the pit with a framework of fragile sticks and then covered these with leaves and straw. Joggemaas Venker suggested that we plant some long sharpened stakes at the bottom of the pit as an extra surprise, but I told him that was not the sort of thing a Godfearing person would do. He was most insistent, so I compromised and let him put in a few short ones.

In the middle of the framework we balanced a small keg of our best muskadel, leaving the stopper out so that the heady fumes of the alcohol would drift into the surrounding forest. At dusk all was set and Joggemaas and I loaded a couple of muskets and climbed up into a nearby tree to wait. We'd brought a couple of sandwiches in case the bait took some time to work.

How wrong we were. Scarcely had the moon risen than we could make them out, dozens of pairs of red eyes peering out of the bush. After half an hour one or two of the braver souls slithered into the open. Obviously they suspected something because they muttered to each other, all the while eyeballing the keg of muskadel.

Obviously the smell was too much for one female. She suddenly plucked up courage and made a dash. Imagine our delight when we saw her scuttle up and try to grab the keg only to find the ground give way underneath her. There was a heavy thud and a scream and then all went silent except for the sounds of her mates speeding back into the bush. Joggemaas cranked off a musket ball in their direction for encouragement.

We climbed down the tree and walked to the pit. We peered down and saw her spreadeagled on a few of the sharpened stakes. Was she writhing in pain? Was she screaming for mercy? Was she dead? Oh, no. She was clutching the keg in both hands, pouring the contents straight down her throat.

"It seems you certainly taught this one a lesson," I said to Joggemaas. "As you can see she's lying there on our stakes clearly regretting the error of her ways."

"We can always hang her tomorrow," he retorted.

As it turned out we couldn't. She was still unconscious and stayed that way for a couple more days. I took pity on her and let her off with only a fifty-minute flogging.

The whole exercise has been a waste of time and effort. There hasn't been the slightest improvement. What we need to do is get to the root of the problem and try to solve it there. I've told Gladys van Thong, one of our social workers, to make contact with the Bergies and show them how to make their own liquor from natural berries and fruits they can pick in the bush. If we can teach them how to do this, they'll no doubt spend the rest of their days smashed and give us far less trouble.

Not much other news. A Portuguese ship dropped in last week. Now you know how I feel about the Portuguese. They're always up to something underhand. The last time they were here we caught some of their men snooping around the vegetable patch asking all sorts of questions and passing disparaging remarks about our brinjals. They seem to think that market gardening is their own special preserve and that no one else should be allowed to try it.

Still, Head Office has insisted that we treat all representatives of other world powers with courtesy. So we had the Captain, an unwashed scoundrel called Mannie da Mavros, around to lunch. What a mistake! Table manners like this you have never seen. He arrived drunk and he left even drunker.

He spent most of the time bragging about what he called the 'Great Portuguese Voyages of Discovery'. Of course everyone knows that these are largely a matter of myth and that in fact nearly all the major sea-routes were first opened by the British and ourselves. But he raved on about how the Portuguese could prove it was them because there were so many Portuguese names all over the place, like Aguada da Saldanha and St Helena Bay and Cape Infante and Angra das Voltas. He claimed that in fact the real name for the Cape itself is Cabo de Tormentosa.

Of course this is all big talk because the da Porroes – as I humorously call them – are still smarting from the licking we gave them in India. They lost a lot of face over there and ever since they've been spreading these wild tales of how the entire world was discovered by them.

One fascinating thing did come out of the lunch. I was telling da Mavros about how we'd tried to sort out our problems with the Bergies. He listened with interest, nodding and belching. Then he told me about a system that a group of Portuguese had worked out up in Mozambique. What they do is employ the local Savages to do all the menial work on their little farms. But instead of paying them, they feed them rations of strong liquor at regular intervals through the day.

"It takes the edge off their natural energy a bit," he said. "But once they're well hooked on the alcohol they'll do anything to get more."

"Including work for it?" I asked.

"Not only work for it, but arrive dead on time every morning so that they can get their morning kicker. They get another mug halfway though the morning's labour, another two at lunchtime and half a bottle each when they knock off. It keeps them just drunk enough so they don't make trouble."

It sounded like a wonderful idea. Of course Maria chipped in and said that she thought such a system was disgusting and that no decent Dutchman would ever dream of doing that sort of frightful thing to his workforce. I suppose she's right but the idea was nice while it lasted.

I must close now. As soon as da Mavros left we noticed a few of the teaspoons and some napkins missing. I want to make sure his ship sails from here without taking the jetty with it.

Congratulations on the promotion. Love to Hendrina.

Yours in God

Van

The Forte de Goede Hoop
January 1657 (?)

Dear Old Hansie

We've just completed a moral clean-up of the settlement.

It started when Cheese Blaauwtjopp marched into the office last Wednesday and dropped a selection of luridly painted cards onto my desk. They depicted the sort of perverted things that take place in some brothels.

"Have you seen these, Commander?"

I glanced through them. They were almost identical to a set that had been passed around by one of the helmsmen on the *Drommedaris* coming out here. "As a matter of fact I have," I said. "And it surprises me, Cheese, that you collect this sort of rubbish."

"Oh, these are not mine, Commander," he said hastily. "I confiscated these from one of the carpenters."

"Well, go and give them back," I said. "They serve a useful purpose with the lower classes, you know. They use these things for private sexual release and if that helps to keep them away from the Hottie womenfolk, all the better."

"If you don't mind me saying so, Commander, you have a lot to learn," he said meaningfully. "I think we might have a little chat about this."

Well, what he told me made my hair stand on end. The problem doesn't involve just a few lewd pictures. There's much else besides. Books and unguents, ointments and artificial devices which do not tolerate description by a Christian. Apparently sailors on Company ships which go to the Far East buy this filth from the Japanese and other depraved Orientals. The sailors then sell this material at a vast profit to other Company employees at the various stops along the route home.

"Are you telling me that they've been selling this sort of stuff right here in the Cape?" I demanded.

"Our settlement is seething with it," said Cheese, wrinkling his nose. "It's high time something was done about it."

I agreed. We couldn't allow this to continue for a day longer. I motioned Cheese to sit down.

"We must think carefully about how to tackle this," I began. "When you start interfering with people's carnal practices you have to be extremely careful where you put your fingers."

"Quite so, Commander."

"It's not going to be just a case of sneaking around the barracks and looking under everyone's mattress for dirty pictures, you know. We're going to have to be very careful so the Hotties don't find out what we're doing. They won't understand."

Cheese nodded. "Mrs van Riebeeck," he said.

"We mustn't let her know either," I agreed.

"No, Commander," he said softly. "I think that Mrs van Riebeeck should be put in charge of this whole investigation."

"Have you gone mad?" I cried. "I'm not having my wife drenching herself in all this smut!"

"But Mrs van Riebeeck would be ideal," said Cheese. "She's an immaculate product of her time. She's upright, narrow-minded, unimaginative, self-righteous, a perfect example of a mid-seventeenth century Dutch woman. Who better to take over the spiritual restructuring of our lonely little community?"

I gaped at him. It had never struck me that way. He went on enthusiastically.

"Commander, I'm sure we both agree that women are best employed in womanly functions like having babies, gossiping and cooking. But colonial Dutch women are not only good at this; they also have an insatiable need to wash everyone else in their own natural purity. I am convinced they were specially designed by the Almighty and put on this earth to keep us on the path of righteousness."

That convinced me. I rushed over immediately to our sleeping quarters. It was only just past eleven so Maria was still snoozing peacefully. I shook her shoulder.

"My darling, I have decided that you are going to take over the moral regrowth of the settlement," I said.

She pulled the pillow over her head.

"I want you to get together a few of your lady friends to help you. I am instructing you to clean up our act," I cried eagerly. "When you are finished I want to know that our little settlement has once and for all been rid of dirty thoughts, lustful ambitions, foul practices and bawdy comic books."

"Please piss off, Van," she muttered.

I lifted the pillow and hissed in her ear. "For the next few weeks I am going to ask you to be selfless. I want you and your lady friends to bring this settlement back to the ways of the Lord."

"What?"

"I want you girls to sneak around this Forte, look under every bed, pick through every hammock, open every book, read every letter, eavesdrop on every secret conversation. I want you to snoop, interfere, meddle, peer, poke, pry and spy. I want you girls to dig out everything in this settlement that is erotic, licentious, off-colour, squalid, grimy, sordid and coarse. In other words, I want you to stick your self-righteous noses deep into other people's groins."

I saw her shiver with excitement. A slow smile spread across her face. "When can we start?" she breathed.

It's the best idea I've ever had. That very afternoon Maria called together two of her friends and they set about their new task in earnest. As I had suspected, I'd touched a sensitive part of their Godly feminine souls. Within hours they started bringing in what they'd confiscated. The problem was far worse than I'd thought.

I looked at the growing pile of pictures, books and pamphlets in the corner of the office.

"You girls are doing a fine job," I said encouragingly as Lettie Groyne staggered in with another boxful. "What's in that one?"

She dumped the box on the floor, looked into it and wrinkled her nose. "I think you rather better have a look yourself, Commander," she said grimly.

I couldn't believe my eyes. I thought the English were depraved. I thought the members of the French courts had gone about as low as a human being can go. I know for a fact the Germans leave everyone standing when it comes to sexual debauchery. But what I saw in that box, Hansie, convinced me that the Orientals have left them all far behind.

I picked up one of the devices which appeared to have been fashioned out of pink rubber. Lettie recoiled in horror.

"Don't touch that, Commander!" she cried.

"Why?"

"It's mine!"

Just then Maria and her other friend, Huddie Truss, entered. They carried two more boxfuls.

"Look at these," she announced with a grimace of disgust, holding up a piece of lady's underclothing of the sort that loose women sport. "Even the womenfolk have acquired this devil's disease."

"We're very pleased you asked us to carry out this work, Commander," said Huddie. "We feel that at last we are being of some real use to this settlement."

"Indeed you are," I replied. "You can leave the rest to us menfolk now. All this unGodly filth will be burned first thing tomorrow morning."

Maria put her hand on my arm. "No, Van," she said quietly. "We won't be burning this stuff yet."

"What?" I protested.

"And we won't be leaving anything for you menfolk to do, either," she continued, adding that nasty edge to her voice. "It's quite clear that you menfolk are not capable of controlling this sort of thing." She gestured at the pile of disgusting pictures, books and pamphlets in the corner of the office.

"But …"

"There are no buts about it," she snapped. "The womenfolk have taken over now."

She and her friends, Lettie and Huddie, glared at me, little smirks on their faces.

"What are you going to do then, bury it?" I asked.

"No, we're not going to bury it either."

She went on to explain that she and her friends had decided that there was only one way to deal with this sort of moral problem and that was by trying to gain a proper understanding of what drove Christian people to indulge in such depravity. She said that, as distasteful as it was, she and her two lady friends were going to make a careful study of all the confiscated disgusting books and pamphlets and devices so that they could be better prepared to deal with any more disgusting books and pamphlets and devices which might come their way in the future.

"Know thine enemy," she said. "It says so in the Bible, Van."

So saying, they loaded up the boxes and staggered off to their quarters. For days there's been much muttering and screams of dismay from behind closed doors. Cheese now thinks that we should have dealt with the matter without involving the ladies. I reminded him that it was his idea that we did.

"I know, Commander. But at that stage I didn't know just how low the depravity in this settlement had sunk. I think confiscating all that repulsive stuff wasn't enough. We should have had a few floggings of the culprits to get the message properly home."

"It's too late for that now," I said. "Maria tells me that she and her friends have carefully examined the odious material. They've done it many times and each time it gets more shocking, more loathsome and more obscene. Yet, try as they can, they still can't understand why Godfearing people would want to possess, let alone read or *use* such appalling examples of the devil's work. So they're gritting their teeth and going through it all again."

"They are very selfless women," I added. "We have to thank God that they agreed to undertake this task on our behalf."

Cheese nodded. "Indeed we do, Commander," he observed.

Nothing else to report this week. Apart from events like the above life is fairly dull and routine. Give my best to the wife and the kids.

Yours in God

Van

The Forte de Goede Hoop
7th April 1657 (?)

My Dear Hansie

I write this at the time of our first great celebration. Yesterday was the fifth anniversary of our landing here at the Cape and we had a bit of a bash to celebrate. It's now three o'clock the following morning and the last of the revellers have finally gone to bed. I'm still quite stoked up and there's no chance that I'd get to sleep, so I'm writing this now.

I kicked off the festivities by holding a good long prayer session and for the first time I allowed the slaves to attend worship at the same time as us. After all, they have put quite a bit of effort into the building of this Forte and in doing much other backbreaking work. I thought it only proper that if we are going to gather and give thanks to the Lord, they might as well be there, too.

Cheese Blaauwtjopp suggested we should take off their chains and leg-irons for the day. I reminded him of the last time we tried doing that, when the heavy rains in the winter of '54 threatened to flood their sleeping-pit. The result was that three of them escaped into the storm and we haven't seen them since.

After prayers we started to frolic in earnest. The soldiers had killed one of these vast river creatures called Hippopotamus and they'd set up a stout framework so that we could cook the giant beast's flesh over an open fire. To keep things merry, I allowed two barrels of rum to be opened. We were very lucky in that Hendryk Boom had just reaped a very fine crop of his stupefying green weeds, so many happy pipes were filled.

In return for a few fragments of copper, the local Khoi-Khoi dance band, The Hottie Seven, agreed to play for the function. A high point in the entertainment was when Tully Slagoffer, one of our leatherworkers, did a turn for us. He put on a frilly yellow dress and gave us his sidesplitting impression of a Portuguese woman trying to pluck her moustache.

The high point for me, of course, was when I gave my speech to thank everyone for all they have put into the settlement, into building the Forte and, in particular, into showing the primitive inhabitants of this end of the African continent how to walk in the virtuous ways of the Lord Almighty. The *Vuildirk* was in harbour again and I was pleased to see that its Captain took interest in what I had to say. I'm sure he'll report back favourably to the Lords Seventeen.

After everyone had eaten well and had had a dance and when the slaves had been safely locked up for the night, Cheese stood up and banged on a saucepan.

"Pray silence," he announced, "for the Commander and spiritual leader of our small settlement: our gracious and honourable and principled master, our Dutchman *extraordinaire*, Jan van Riebeeck."

There were a few hoarse cheers as I mounted the small platform. I looked down at the sea of happy, expectant faces.

"I'm going to use this occasion," I began, "to speak to you about the wonderful work that you have been doing and will continue to do in this far-flung outpost of the civilised world."

I could see a couple of yawns so I hastened on.

"A lot of you," I said, "believe that you were sent here merely as employees of the Dutch East India Company, that you were sent here merely to be gardeners and soldiers, that you were sent here merely to build a Forte and man it. But on the fifth anniversary of our stay here, I want to remind you that you were sent here for far more than that. You were sent here to be the representatives of God's Love."

"Get to the point, Van!" Maria hissed at me from behind the platform.

"I want to remind you of the first great story in the Holy Bible," I said, letting my voice get a bit wobbly with emotion. "In that story it tells how one day in Heaven, God decided to make the first man, Adam, in His own image. When He had finished making Adam, He looked at him and saw that he was good. And then God put Adam on the new world that God had also just made.

"So Adam was not only the first man on earth, he was the first colonist," I said.

That line got a great round of applause. I smiled down at them.

"You, too, are colonists," I said. "And you have every reason to feel proud of that. Colonists are the people God chose to carry His word and His righteousness into the far-flung outposts of the world. You are here to set a magnificent example to the pagan hordes, to show by your actions and Christian compassion that you are truly God's children."

As I descended from the platform I could see that my point had got home because there were visible tears in the eyes of many. I found myself slapped on the back many times by members of the staff who told me that my little speech had made them feel it had all been worth it.

The party really got under way then with more dancing and singing and leaping about. Just after one o'clock Maria, who'd been having quite a serious talk with the rum, passed out. I slung her over my shoulder, bade everyone goodnight and, in a jovial frame of mind, retired to our sleeping chamber.

My bliss wasn't to last very long. As I was undressing Maria, the Provost Marshall banged on the door. He'd come to tell me that the Sergeant-at-Arms, Jackson Dieselgat, had just been caught behind the western rampart copulating with one of the Company's prize watermelons. While he was having his fruity pleasure, four of his men took the opportunity to desert, first raiding the vegetable garden so they had supplies for their journey. They'd made off with about three hundred of our turnips, two cows and a pig.

"Get some men together and go after them first thing in the morning," I told the Provost Marshall crossly.

"What must I do with the Sergeant-at-Arms?"

"Slap him in irons for the night. We'll give him a few dozen lashes tomorrow."

"Would you like me to throw the watermelon away?"

I thought for a moment. "No," I said. "There's bound to be an English or Portuguese ship in here one of these days whining for provisions. We'll tell them it got dropped on a marlin spike."

And thus did we bring to a close our first five years in this place. I can't say that I'm delighted with the way it's all turned out, but on the other hand, I can't say that it's been a total waste of time. Head Office have asked me to stay on another five years but I think that's going to be it as far as I'm concerned. I so long for the Far East again. Apart from all its mysteries, it has a far better class of pagan.

All my love to Hennie and the ankle-biters.

Yours in God

Van

My Dear Hansie

We had our first squatter problem last week.

No one knows where they came from or why. But one day there was a piece of open windswept land on the southern side of the Forte with nothing on it except a few straggly grey bushes. The next morning we woke up and found that three or four hundred Savages had moved in. Overnight they'd built a village, using old sacks and bits of packing-cases and animal skins and anything else they could lay their thieving hands on.

I sent for the man in charge of Dutch-Savage liaison, Sergeant Buyer Hardegatt.

"Would you like to explain to me what all this is about?" I demanded. "We can't have these creatures camping out on our doorstep. Firstly, they smell. Secondly, they're a security risk. Thirdly, if they stay there it's going to bring down the value of the Forte."

"I didn't know anything about it myself, Commander," he whined. "They didn't tell me anything about it."

"Well, what do you intend to do about it?"

He shrugged. "It's really quite simple, Commander. We must go and burn down their dwellings and grab a few of the leaders and shoot them. The rest of them will soon get the message and move out."

"Have you gone mad?" I cried. "In case you hadn't noticed, there's a Portuguese ship in the bay. If they see us shooting indigenes you can be damned sure they'll sail back to Europe and run around telling everyone that Dutch colonists are nothing but a crowd of inhuman capitalistic thugs. They'll say that we're ruthlessly exploiting the Noble Savages to the point of wholesale murder."

"I thought that's what we were supposed to be doing."

"But we're not supposed to advertise it," I snarled.

"Well, what do we do?"

I smiled at him. "We do what all inhuman capitalistic colonial thugs do when they're in a tight spot with Noble Savages. We negotiate."

"Negotiate?"

"Negotiate. It's a fancy word for being slimy. We get their leaders in here and we show them a bit of the old Dutch double-tongue."

He looked doubtful. I told him to start by seeing that extra guards were put on all the livestock, in the vegetable patch and on anything else that wasn't nailed down. Once he'd done that I told him to go and talk to the squatters, tell them to elect a spokesman and send him up to see me.

"And tell them to dig some lavatory pits in the meantime," I yelled after him. "Tell them I've heard of squatting but this is ridiculous."

"I still think we should just shoot them," he yelled back.

Just after three o'clock that afternoon Cheese Blaauwtjopp announced that a Chief Banjoman Koyle would like to see me and should he first confiscate the Chief's spears, shield, hatchet, hunting knives and clubs.

"What's he want to bring those in here for?"

"He says they're part of his cultural heritage," said Cheese with a sneer.

I told him to load up a couple of our cultural muskets and lean them against the desk where they'd be clearly visible.

The Chief announced himself as 'the democratically elected leader of the squatters'. I told him that while we understood that his people had problems, we simply couldn't allow them to move onto Company property when they felt like it. I said that I expected him to be responsible and lead his people back into the bleak wastelands where they belong. I said that we'd be quite prepared to help them move and we'd donate some extra building materials by way of encouragement.

As it turned out he wasn't nearly as easy to bamboozle as I thought he'd be. He said that ever since white men had arrived in this country, life had become intolerable for the Savages. He claimed white men had been tearing around the place shooting all the Savage's wild animals, giving them worthless beads in return for their cattle, fumbling with their women, dumping poisons into their streams, poking fun at their witchdoctors, burning down their forests, planting alien vegetation and generally turning all the Savage's traditional values into a ball of shit. He said they had no option but to move close to the white man's settlement where at least they could look for work.

"It's actually all your fault," he finished.

I said I'd think about what he had to say and sent him on his way. Afterwards I spoke to Cheese. As usual he was full of advice.

"It's up to you, Commander," he said. "But I tend to agree with Sergeant Hardegatt. You can't afford to be soft with these creatures. Before you know what's happened the word will get out and you'll find the Forte surrounded by them."

"What do you suggest?"

He smiled. "They want work, let's give them work. Since the dysentery epidemic we're a bit short on slaves anyway."

"In case you'd forgotten, we're not supposed to take slaves from the locals," I snapped. "Head Office says that they must be captured in faraway places like Angola so they don't try to run away."

"Who will know the difference?" he said. "One Savage is much like another."

"And what about the Chief?" I asked.

"Oh, that's quite easy. We lock him up."

"Lock him up?"

"Lock him up. Detain him. Incarcerate him. Dump him in the dungeons and throw away the key."

"We can't just imprison him," I protested.

"It's not imprisonment, Commander. Rather think of it as sentencing him to a term of self-improvement."

Basically I didn't like his idea but I could certainly see the merit in it.

"Keep talking," I said.

"Commander, you must try to think in the long term. The white man is in this country to stay. If you are tough now, you will sort out the squatter problem once and for all. You will go down in history as a visionary."

That made up my mind. I told Cheese to organise things. Five minutes after the Portuguese ship had disapppeared over the horizon we had Chief Banjoman Koyle safely under lock and key. We sent a couple of heavy wagons to the squatter camp and flattened the dwellings. Hardegatt personally castrated a couple of the Savages as a warning. The rest of them got the message and slithered back into the wilderness.

I told Cheese I felt a bit guilty. "If news of this ever does get back to Europe," I wondered, "is there any way we can say we were just being good Christians?"

"It's already been taken care of, Commander. When we threw the Chief into the dungeons, we threw a Bible in after him."

I must say the Chief's cultural weapons look good. I've had them mounted on the office wall. I've told the soldiers to keep an eye out for any other primitive artefacts they might come across when they meet up with Savages on their forays over the mountains. Spears and drums and shields and head-dresses and so on. I thought we could set up a little shop here and flog these to passing ships. There isn't an able seaman who comes past here who doesn't want to take a little bit of Africa back with him.

Maria says we shouldn't even bother with getting them from the Savages. We're quite capable of making cheap copies our-selves. The tourists will never know the difference.

Not much other news except that we're having a meeting of the Council this afternoon to decide on appropriate punishment for one of our male sick-comforters, Nils Vagus. The disgusting little bastard was caught at three o'clock one morning having sexual congress with a sheep. The Sergeant-at-Arms heard this frightful bleating and rushed down to the hornwork thinking that some wild animal had got into the enclosure. Instead there was Vagus, getting to the short strokes. The Sergeant-at-Arms said that what disturbed him was that the sheep appeared to be enjoying it just as much as its molester was.

Cheese says we must remember that it was a Hottentot sheep and that he'd heard that for centuries these animals have been carefully trained to behave in a passionate fashion whenever they see a lonely man. Therefore, he said, we shouldn't put all the blame on Vagus as the sheep probably put him up to it. I know that in Batavia some of the Javanese Savages had taught a jungle tree-ape to perform sexual acts, but I think that was just for entertainment. I mean it wasn't part of their tradition.

Notwithstanding all that, I think we're going to have to make an example of the ardent Mr Vagus. If the word gets around that we've been lenient, who knows what could happen. I'm going to recommend a fairly severe keelhaul or two. I've found that dropping before the yardarm isn't having the necessary deterrent effect any more.

Give my best to Hennie.

Yours in God

Van

The Forte de Goede Hoop
November 1657 (?)

My Dear Hansie

We've got ourselves a new maid. I cannot tell you what a relief to get rid of the last one, Rina, who had raised the art of cunning theft to new heights.

It all came to a head when I paid a surprise visit to her hovel one Saturday morning. I often do that sort of thing so that the Hottie staff know we have their interests at heart. What was the first thing to greet my eyes? Lounging under a knopdoring tree was her layabout husband, Plaaitjies, dressed in one of my best jackets and wearing one of my favourite auburn wigs. I can tell you, I was more than slightly annoyed. The annoyance grew when I noticed he was also wearing a pair of my best shoes on his feet.

I fired Rina on the spot and told the pair of them to report to Godjong Cloete on Monday morning for a really pensive flogging. Obviously I can't take the clothes back now that he's used them, so all I can do is hope that this new maid is going to be a bit better. I've told Maria to tighten up on domestic security.

The new maid is called Monica Droop and she seems a cut above her sisters, although that isn't saying much. Maria says she came with very good recommendations from Beverley and Gary Benecke who've been transferred to Malaya. In fact they wanted to take her with them but Head Office policy doesn't allow this. That policy is actually a pain in the arse because when these indigenes come to you they don't even know how to hold a broom. People like the Beneckes spend months training them, teaching them to speak Dutch and trying to bring them into the light of the Lord. And then Head Office claims that we don't have any moral right to drag our Hottie servants all over the world with us!

Anyway, we're lucky in the sense that at least we don't have to start from scratch with Monica. She's done her basics so I have high hopes. Otherwise she looks just like the rest of them in that she's had her front upper teeth pulled out. Maria asked her why they all had this done.

"Is it some sort of primitive belief?" she said.

"No, Madam, I take them out so I can try to speak better to God."

"Don't be ridiculous, my girl," said Maria. "Your front teeth don't get in the way when you're speaking to God."

"It's your evil Hottie mind that gets in the way," I added humorously.

"Master?" she enquired.

"Never mind."

Maria bombed all over me later for what she called my lack of sensitivity. She often does this so that she can feel she's keeping me in my place.

"Why do you always have to speak to these people in such a rough fashion?" she demanded. "They also have feelings, you know. They also have their little hopes and joys. Why do you have to make such cruel fun of them?"

"The only hopes they have are whether they can find something else to steal," I breezed. "And their only joy is when they succeed."

God help us when a woman gets an idea inside her empty head, especially if that idea is that she's going to change someone else for the better. I thought it was only the Almighty who was supposed to make people in His own image. Not so, I'm afraid. In the households of this world there are hundreds of thousands of anxious womenfolk desperately trying to turn their servants into copies of themselves. I suppose it's something to do with women being an inferior version of men. They always have this need to seek out someone more unfortunate than themselves onto whom they can then dump all the charity and compassion they should be saving up for their husbands.

Maria took great pains in the further instruction of Monica Droop. She's taught her all manner of white people's more genteel habits, like how to talk without using so many swear words, how to dress modestly, how to stand up and bow when a man enters the room, how to wash her hands before going to the privy, how to lift her little finger when scratching and so on. I told Maria to make sure that she also teaches her to drive her atavistic reproductive instincts deep down into her subconscious so that she doesn't go on breeding as prolifically as her Hottie sisters.

I got a little cross when I found out that Monica was being taught to read as well.

"What on earth makes you think that is necessary?" I asked.

"The indigenes have as much right to learning as we do," Maria replied with a toss of her head. "Isn't that one of the things we Dutch people are supposed to be doing, bringing civilisation to the dark continents?"

"That's what they like to say in the Fatherland," I said. "The Lords Seventeen like to give the impression that they aren't out here simply to rape and pillage every new country for every penny it's worth. They put out these stories that they're really out here to bring civilisation to the unhappy pagan hordes. It goes down terribly well and makes everyone feel better, gives them something to talk about at the opera. It's called public relations."

I could have been explaining to a wall. Anyway, I have to admit that in some ways Monica is turning out far better than her predecessor. I would have left it at that except things went wrong when Jaegel Vommitt came to dinner one Tuesday. He's the new Powder Store Manager they sent out to replace Gary Benecke. He took one look at Monica Droop and you could see there was going to be trouble. I tackled Maria about it as soon as he'd left.

"Did you see that?" I cried. "Did you see the way he was looking at her? Did you see how she was fluttering her eyelashes at him? This is all your fault."

"So, what's wrong with that?" She was all innocence.

"What's wrong with it! I'll tell you what's wrong with it, madam. Before you can say Dutch East India Company those two are going to be in each other's arms rubbing their bacon together. Did you see the way she loosened her bodice and let it hang open when she was serving him the broth?"

"I thought it was rather sweet," she said. "The trouble with you, Van, is you're getting old. You can't remember what it's like to be full of lust and desire."

That may be so, but what Maria doesn't realise is that if I let this thing run its course there's no telling what could happen. It has always been my policy to try to keep the staff away from the Hottie women. I've told you before about the disgraceful behaviour of certain of the military who had been making free with the Hottie womenfolk. And some of them had started fooling around with the Savage womenfolk as well. Last year one of them, a young cadet, had actually run away and set up home in a skin hut with a Bushwoman. I'd had to arrange quite a few floggings, keelhaulings and droppings before the yardarm to get that all back under control. And here was my own wife encouraging the same kind of perverse behaviour under my own roof.

A week later I called Jaegel Vommitt into the office. I had Cheese Blaauwtjopp in as a witness and I gave Vommitt a very stern lecture on the matter, thinking that would put an end to things. He didn't seem too impressed so I showed him some of the entries in the Punishment Book. It had no effect. He just sniffed.

"We must follow where our hearts lead us, Commander. Monica and I have had a long chat about it and we're quite prepared for the consequences of the enduring love for each other which is blossoming in our hearts."

"Come here, Vommit," I said. He reluctantly followed me as I walked over to the window. I pointed down into the parade ground.

"You see that row of men down there, the ones all chained together emptying out that pit lavatory with their teeth? Those men are called slaves and I wouldn't say they have a lot of job satisfaction."

He peered down. "So?"

"So, if you look at number three and number five along the chain, you'll see that they've got slightly lighter complexions than the others. Those two are a couple of Dutchmen who took it upon themselves to discharge themselves from the service of the Company and try to walk back to the Fatherland. Shame. They've been there a whole year and they're going to be there a whole year more."

"So?"

"So, all I'm saying is that if you are looking for an interesting sexual life I can guarantee one for you. Being chained to seventeen Guinea Savages for twenty-four hours a day can be most instructional in matters of the groin."

That took the smug grin off his face.

"I'm not a man to be fooled with," I told him.

"No, he isn't," added Cheese. "You must listen to what the Commander tells you and keep your covetous fingers off the indigenous womenfolk."

After Vommitt had slunk away I thanked Cheese for his support.

"I hope you realise it's not going to do any good, Commander," he said. "No matter how much you threaten and bluster, you can't put a brake on people's lustful desires. It's like Socrates said: When the penis stands up, the brains fall on the ground."

"What are we going to do?" I asked bitterly.

"There's only one thing to do," he said. "You are going to have to pass a law making it a punishable offence for white men to copulate with Hotties or Savages. And write in a really stiff penalty for anyone who breaks that law. It's the only way."

"They'll never sit still for something like that," I growled. "You can do anything to a Dutchman. You can send him all over the world to live in pagan countries. You can pay him monkey's wages. You can swindle him and maltreat him and abuse him. You can do virtually anything you like with him. There's only one thing you must never do and that's try to tell him what he can stick his schlong into."

"Then we must find a biblical precedent, Commander. I'm sure if we really scour the Bible we'll find something carelessly said by one of those pessimistic First Testament prophets and which can be distorted to fit our needs. We've often done that before."

What he proposed was, of course, a wonderful idea. There's nothing like the weight of the Bible behind decisions you know are going to be wildly unpopular. Whenever anyone whinges about them you can always raise your eyes mournfully towards Heaven, put your hand over your heart and say that you're only fulfilling God's Eternal Design.

In this case God's Eternal Design was expressed perfectly in Exodus 20, Verse 17. He could have written it specially for the occasion. I read it out to Cheese.

"Thou shalt not covet thy neighbour's houses, thou shalt not covet thy neighbour's wife, nor his manservant, nor his maidservant, nor his ox nor his ass, nor anything that is thy neighbour's."

"I like that bit about the maidservant," I said to Cheese. "Couldn't have said it better myself."

"Very good, Commander. It warns them to keep their hands off each other's asses, too."

"You could always add that bit from Leviticus," I said. "The one where it says thou shalt not sow thy field with mingled seed."

"Once again you are going to go down in history as a visionary, Commander," said Cheese rather nicely as we rubbed our hands together and got down to drafting the proposed new Godfearing legislation. "With this brilliant tactic you will, for all time, have saved the Dutchman from himself."

In the interim I've had Monica Droop delivered to Robben Island where she'll have plenty of time to reflect on her wanton desires as she picks her way through all the penguin turds. What a wonderful find that island has been.

In the meantime we've taken on a temp called Eva. She's a niece of that unsavoury little fink Hottentot Harry, so we'd better be careful and keep a sharp eye on her.

Lots of love to Hennie and the brats.

Yours in God

Van

My Dear Old Hansie

I'm getting very worried about Cheese Blaauwtjopp. He seems to have gone a bit soft. I don't know what's caused it, but it's probably a combination of the long years away from home and his not ever having got married. His loneliness has had its penalties and for the last year or so he's not been behaving at all like a reliable Dutchman. All the things they carefully inculcated into him at the Leiden Colonial Institute seem to have gone by the board. He still comes to prayers – he's not that far gone – but he doesn't join in with other activities any more, preferring to sulk in his quarters. He's reading far too many books, he's started saying things that he actually means and, worst of all, I haven't seen him at a Hottie-flogging in months.

Take the matter of my Forestry Clearance Plan. As I think I've told you, most of this place has these great dense woodlands stretching for miles in every direction. They make me very nervous because of what's hiding in them. They need to be removed or we'll never feel completely safe. Normally I would expect Cheese to back me up on something like this. Instead I got exactly the opposite reaction when I announced that we were going to spend the next year or two chopping down trees on a serious basis. He was full of complaint.

"But, Commander," he protested, "you can't go around destroying the forests. They are lovely and important. They are full of tentative birdsong, gentle fruits and flowers, gaudy butterflies and larks, sweet tumbling streams and hidden glades with bunny rabbits and all manner of little furry creatures. God's creatures."

"They are also full of centipedes, scorpions, snakes and Savages," I snapped. "Take a walk in your famous forests and take a look up any Maroela tree. You'll find it's swarming with Griquas and Namas all armed to the teeth. The forests are a security risk and they have to go!"

From the expression on his face I thought he was going to start weeping. It's quite amazing how much resistance there is these days to any idea with a bit of foresight attached to it. If we cut down all the forests we can use the space to plant more vegetables. With no trees there'll be no foliage in the way so we'll be able to send signals to each other from the hilltops. Best of all, when you've got no trees you can see any advancing pagan hordes when they're still miles away. You have simply got to put common sense before sentimentality, I always say. But try telling that to the Cheese Blaauwtjopps of this world.

"Commander," he said, his voice quivering, "those forests have been there since time immemorial. They have taken thousands and thousands of years to develop. They are a fountain of life, a part of the earth's heritage, a complex and wondrous celebration of life in both spectacular and humble revelation."

"You've seen one forest, you've seen them all," I retorted with humour. Then I let my face darken with authority. "And there will be no further argument about this, Cheese. We are going to chop the forests down or set fire to them. I won't be happy until I see this country barren and windswept, lashed mercilessly by bitter rain and cold, not a tree in sight."

"Just like Holland?" he sneered.

I told him not to be sarcastic and he went off muttering. I don't know what I'm going to do with him. I suggested he might like to go back to Leiden for a refresher course at the Institute, but he refused to entertain the idea. I like the idea because while he's in Holland he might well pick up a wife for himself, someone who could come back out here and keep him company.

We had a couple of passing missionaries here last week. Most of these God-botherers come from England so it was surprising and pleasant to see a couple of Dutchmen instead. They were on their way to Cochin China to spread the Word to the barbarians there, but they said that Head Office asked them to have a peep around at the Cape as they passed to see how our spiritual welfare was surviving.

They were particularly impressed by some of the facts I was able to give them, especially when it came to the examples I gave of the deep way in which Christian behaviour was practised at the settlement.

"We have prayers every day at six sharp," I told them. "And no one is allowed to miss these unless they have an acceptable excuse, like they were out on a Hottie shoot or had some slaves to flog."

"Do you find you have to shoot a lot of these Hottentots?" the taller one asked.

"Not as many as we used to," I admitted. "And it depends on the time of the year. If it's winter they tend to do a lot more stealing than in the fruitful months. But I have to admit that by and large they don't seem to be getting the message about it being unGodly to thieve."

The conversation then moved on to the matter of conversions. They were both very interested to learn how many Savages and Hotties we had managed to bring to the ways of the Lord. I explained that it wasn't as easy as it sounded and that before we could even talk to these creatures about such matters, we first had to convince them that we had a right to be in this country."

"I can't understand why but they seem to harbour a great resentment of us," I explained.

"Good Heavens, I can't imagine why," said the taller one. "Surely you have told them of all the benefits you will bring to them?"

"Yes, I have," I cried. "I have told them that this isn't the first time that God has dispatched His Love to their benighted continent. Many centuries earlier His Love was generously bestowed upon Egypt. On that occasion the Egyptians had a season or two of pestilences that would put their own problems to shame. Plagues of flies were delivered upon them. No sooner had the flies disappeared than a new plague appeared over the horizon in the form of battalions of frogs. Then God sent them locusts and floods and death of the firstborn, and then, to round it all off, everyone got boils.

"To this end of Africa He sent the Dutchman," I finished off.

"And how did they respond?" asked the shorter one.

"While I was talking, two of them sneaked around behind me and stole my umbrella," I said sourly.

They said that was very sad but it showed that we were clearly not putting enough effort into battering Christian values into the poor ignorants God had put in our way. They said He would be most disappointed if we didn't make a better job of spreading His Word. I said they should come and spend more than a few days here and they'd soon learn that that wasn't as easy as it sounded. They went off muttering.

I don't know whether I've told you much about this new Company Surgeon we've been lumbered with. I think he must have learned his finer medical techniques in an abattoir. Old Fransie de Wijkkedlijeeq had a small whitlow on his index finger. He went to see Sawbones du Plessis who poured half a gallon of rum down his throat and then proceeded to cut off his entire arm! I've had a touch of the old Batavia Rumbles recently and I'm terrified to go near the man. Who knows what he'll do.

Must rush. We're selling off some used slaves and I want to see that they're properly searched before they go.

All best regards to the family.

Yours in God

Van

My Dear Old Hansie

Once you've read this letter I want you to burn it. Normally I wouldn't tell anyone what I'm going to tell you because I simply cannot risk this sort of story getting out. But I just have to get it off my chest. Who better than to an old mate I can trust?

The whole ghastly business began when a small party of soldiers went in pursuit of a party of Strandlopers who'd got a bit close to the settlement. As you may remember, these Strandlopers are the itinerant Hottie sub-species who live by scavenging the shoreline and anything else they happen to pass by, like vegetables and goats and cattle and other desirable goodies to be found near white people's Fortes. For these reasons we like to keep them at a distance. So, whenever they come skulking up the beach, I dispatch a small armed platoon in their direction.

Everything would have been all right except the corporal in charge of the platoon decided to chase the Strandlopers deep into the beachside undergrowth where they have their little encampments. Most of them disappeared into the foliage except for one nursing mother who couldn't run fast enough.

The soldiers were fascinated when they found out what she was carrying under her arm. It appeared to be a baby of about six months, healthy except for the fact that, when they looked closely, they found out it had three legs.

If that wasn't bad enough, our Company Surgeon, Sawbones du Plessis, has had this baby brought in here to the Forte. When I heard about it I went down to the clinic immediately.

"I don't want that baby in here," I told him. "It's not right."

"Why not?"

"Because babies with three legs are unnatural," I replied tersely. "Now either have it returned to its mother or, better still, take it outside and put it out of its misery."

"We've got the mother here, too," he replied calmly, pointing to a corner of the ward. There she was, sitting on a bed of our best sacking as if she owned it. She waved and flung a gap-toothed smile in my direction.

"And I think before you make those sort of decisions you should have a look at this baby, Commander," Sawbones continued. "It's a discovery of scientific importance."

"It's got nothing to do with scientific importance," I sniffed. "That baby is nothing more than a frightening example of the devil's work. And the sooner you realise that the better. The next thing we'll have is Savages with four arms and Bushmen with an extra eye."

"Come and look at it, Commander."

"I don't want to see it, thank you," I snapped. "I've seen plenty of those sort of things at Amsterdam fairgrounds."

There was a tap on my arm. Cheese Blaauwtjopp had slunk in quietly. "I think what Doctor du Plessis is trying to say, Commander, is that this baby might represent an important new evolutionary step."

"Are you trying to say that a three-legged Hottie baby is an example of God's work?" I demanded. "Just you be careful, young man. I won't have blasphemy. You could find yourself undergoing a quick whipping for that sort of opinion."

Cheese smiled. "Quite the opposite, Commander," he said smoothly. "If God had made this creature it would be perfect, just like a Dutch baby. It would have two legs, bluish-green eyes, flowing hair, a pale white skin and a moderately sized wee-wee. But you see, Commander, God doesn't have the time any more to see to every last little thing in Heaven and earth. It's all become just too much for one man. Now and then He has to leave Mother Nature to get on with things on her own. And sometimes Mother Nature has to have quite a few tries before she gets it right.

"Which is probably how the Portuguese and the English came into being," he added.

I couldn't argue with that. "So what are you trying to say?" I asked.

Sawbones put his arm around my shoulder. "What we think we have discovered here, Commander, is an example of a completely new kind of creature which has been designed specially to be able to make the best use of its surroundings. Think of the camel, Commander. The camel has got two great humps on its back in which it carries its water for the long journeys it has to make across the desert. It has adapted to its environment."

The horror of what they were telling me gradually sank in. The Strandlopers had obviously produced a new improved model of themselves. I could just see it. These creatures already have these great flat dishlike feet for running away from us on the beach. If they all started growing three legs we'd never catch them.

"So what are you suggesting?" I whispered to Sawbones.

"We're suggesting that we make careful enquiries to find out whether this is the only three-legged Strandloper there is, or whether there are lots of others."

"Now do you understand?" said Cheese unnecessarily.

I told them I'd like to think it over. That evening I told Maria about it. Her reaction wasn't what I thought it would be.

"All I can say is why can't you people just leave the poor little thing alone?" she complained. "It's not harming anyone."

I snorted. "Can you imagine what harm this could do to my career? People running around in Amsterdam saying, 'Have you heard about Jan van Riebeeck and his three-legged Hottie?' I'll become a laughing stock."

"So let them say it. What can they do?" she sneered.

"And have you considered what the Lords Seventeen will think if they ever find out about this?" I asked. "They hate this sort of scandal at Head Office. They've got their image to think of. We'll find ourselves shipped back to Holland and kicked out of the Company."

She sighed heavily. "You're not being logical, Van. You're letting your emotions run away with you."

"I've been kicked out of this Company once before," I reminded her bitterly. "And I had to eat seventeen roods of Lordly shit to get my job back."

Again she gave her patronising sigh.

"Whatsmore," I continued, "if news of this gets to the church elders in the Fatherland, they will certainly kick up a fuss. You know what they're like. I could get excommunicated or something."

"You can't get excommunicated, Van. You're a Dutch Protestant. The worst they can do is give you a severe bollocking."

"Thanks a lot," I said.

That evening at Bible Class I decided to ask for some real help. Instead of leading the prayers in my fine clear baritone, I loped off into a corner, fell to my knees and had a few private words with a Certain Someone. At least when I ask Him for help He doesn't give me so much uphill.

The next day I told Cheese to see that Sawbones had the three-legged Hottie baby and its mother moved out of the clinic.

"Tell him that for the meantime they can stay in Hottentot Harry's shack in the stockade under the western rampart," I instructed.

"Have you asked Hottentot Harry about this?" he enquired.

"I don't have to ask Hottentot Harry about anything," I snapped. "And in case you hadn't noticed he was sent back to Robben Island last week to further reflect on his English-acquired ways."

"Oh," was all he could think to say.

Two nights later at about three in the morning a fierce lion carried away both the three-legged Hottie and its mother. Of course it was sheer coincidence that the Sergeant-at-Arms, Jackson Dieselgat, had left the stockade gates open. Mysterious are the ways of the Lord.

I'll finish this now. As I look out of the window I can see the longboats getting ready to take the last bits and pieces out to the *Vuildirk* before she sails north, so I want to catch the post.

Give my best to Hendrina and the kiddies.

Yours in God

Van

The Forte de Goede Hoop
13th February 1659

My Dear Hansie

Those whom the gods would destroy they first make randy.

A terrible new pestilence has arrived in the Cape. I don't know whether you've heard about this frightful scourge, but it's a real downer. It is called Syphilis and it is spread by sexual congress but apparently only when this sexual congress takes place outside holy matrimony. I hope for your sake it never gets to Europe.

No one knows where Syphilis comes from, but our Company Surgeon, Sawbones du Plessis, has come up with one of his typically extravagant medical theories. He claims it all started with baboons. According to Sawbones, Syphilis is natural to the baboons. Once they catch it, though, they immediately develop luminous blue arses as a warning to other baboons not to fool around. What happened was that up in Mossel Bay a couple of the local Savages got fearfully drunk one night. As they were groping their way home to their huts they came across a particularly attractive female baboon caught in a trap. You can guess what then went on. Having had their way with the baboon, they went on home to their wives.

A few weeks later a southbound DEIC supply ship dropped in to Mossel Bay for water. As is the tradition, some of the deckhands got shoreleave and made free with the local Savage womenfolk. The rest is history.

Sawbones says that if you get Syphilis you can lean over and kiss your dick goodbye. There's no known cure and there never will be. It takes a long time to kill you, too – up to twenty years! What is worse, for all that time you don't even know you've got it. Apparently in humans the buttocks stay exactly the same colour so there's simply no warning.

I didn't know what to do at first but after a quick ponder I realised that I could turn this whole thing to my advantage. I immediately launched a campaign throughout the settlement saying that the disease was obviously a sign from Heaven. I pointed out that clearly God was angry with us over our sexually reckless behaviour. I said that the message had been handed down to mankind on several previous occasions. When the ancient God warned them in many ways and when they still didn't listen He sent them a flood. On this occasion we were being given a warning to get our morals in order once and for all.

You can imagine the rapture with which this opinion was received in the settlement. That sanctimonious hypocrite, André de Flaggyl, stopped me in the passage.

"It's typical," he said prissily. "Whenever anything goes wrong around here you immediately try to blame it all on God."

"Well, where do *you* think it came from?"

He smiled nastily. "Why, Commander, it came from certain staff members in your happy little Forte."

"Who?"

"Don't be so naive, Commander. Surely you've noticed them? Jacoby Branquette and his friend Mark Pistoris?" He put his head on one side and let one of his wrists go limp.

"I don't know what you're talking about," I said.

He shook his head. "Commander," he said quietly, "I think we'd better go to your office and have a little chat. It's time someone told you about some of the unexpected facts of life."

What he described was the most outrageous thing I think I've ever heard. At first I couldn't believe it, but he insisted it was true. And it isn't only Branquette and Pistoris. According to de Flaggyl, there are several other male staff members who are indulging in this depraved behaviour.

I was deeply shocked, Hansie. It's the sort of degenerate conduct I could accept if someone came along and said it was practised among the Bushmen or some of the more backward Savages, even the occasional Hottentot.

"I simply can't believe white men would do this sort of thing," I said coldly.

"This is the seventeenth century, Commander," he said smugly. "All sorts of new and scandalous things are taking place."

"Are you trying to tell me that two men actually go into a room somewhere, take off all their clothes, climb into the hammock and then ..?" Words failed me.

He nodded.

I shook my head in disbelief. "And I thought Branquette and Pistoris were just good friends," I said. "All that hugging and holding hands and playing with each other's hair. That's why I let them share sleeping quarters."

Again he nodded. He really seemed to be enjoying the way he was upsetting me. I shook my finger at him.

"But Dr du Plessis told me that it all started with baboons who passed it on to the Savages who then passed it on to the human race."

"Obviously he was wrong," he retorted.

"So you're saying that this dreadful scourge comes from male members of the Forte staff? There are no baboons involved?"

"Not so far," he said with a smirk.

I remembered that when I was in Batavia we had a similar problem when a couple of the slaves were caught being over-affectionate with the Company's chickens. But we sorted that out by cutting off their heads. Unfortunately, we had to kill the chickens, too. But I wasn't prepared to go to those lengths on this occasion so what I've done is appoint Piston Velrash's wife, Rita, as Chief Medical Adviser. She's about as talented as a lounge curtain but I know I can rely on her to be both merciless and discreet. I'm terrified that reports of this disgrace might get back to Head Office even though André de Flaggyl tells me I needn't worry about that because this sort of odious sexual behaviour has been going on in Holland for years. Sometimes I'm pleased I'm old-fashioned.

On a happier note. Ever since we imported these new dogs from Germany there's been a marked decrease in theft from the vegetable garden. There's also been a marked decrease in wildlife, including one or two Strandlopers. Still, I suppose one has to take the good with the bad.

Love to Hennie and the crawlers.

Yours in God

Van

The Forte de Goede Hoop
26th April 1659

My Dear Old Hansie

I was quite excited for a while when Cheese Blaauwtjopp came up with one of his sporadic good ideas. He said that what we need in the settlement is some sort of National Anthem, some stirring song that we could all stand up and sing together heartily on important occasions. He said it would serve to make us proud of ourselves. Get our spirits up when things were going bad.

As I say, I was quite chuffed with the idea. So I asked Cheese to look around for a suitable tune and some stirring words to go with it. I know that a few members of the Forte staff brought lutes and Jewish harps out here. Maybe one of them could come up with a catchy refrain.

I couldn't have been more wrong. The next day Buckle Zsamfoort, one of the cobblers, came up to see me. He said he wanted to sing me a song he'd composed and which would fit the bill nicely. He'd brought along one of his acne-strewn apprentices who accompanied him on a French twelve-string zither. Zsamfoort stood at one side of the office with his hands on his hips and after much clearing of the throat burst into song in his leatherlike voice. The tune was unspeakable and I couldn't believe the words. It started off:

> The baboon climbs the mountain
> So hastily and so awkwardly,
> The baboon climbs the mountain
> So hastily and so awkwardly,
> The baboon climbs the mountain
> In order to irritate the farmers;
> Hooray for the jolly baboon.

"You can stop right there, Buckle," I said. "It's not what we're looking for."

"What's wrong with it?" he expostulated irascibly.

"For a start I've made it quite clear we are looking for a National Anthem. Something to make us proud of what we are and what we stand for. It is supposed to be about noble and self-sacrificing Dutch people," I said as pleasantly as I could manage. "It is not meant to be about baboons."

"You said you wanted a merry song," he protested.

"Quite," I said, still trying to sound reasonable. "Your little song is indeed very merry, but let's say it's not what we're looking for."

When he'd left Cheese Blaauwtjopp brought in the next bundle of local musical talent. Apparently he had them lined up outside the office. This one turned out to be Beulah Cloete, the flat-chested wife of our Chief Flogger. She's a scungie little female with a body odour that would flatten a helmsman. She wears her hair in long greasy braids and festoons herself with Bushman beads. She started by trying to creep up my arse with all sorts of obvious flattery about how wonderful it was that the settlement had such a culturally aware Commander and how privileged she felt at the chance to contribute to the spiritual upliftment of the Forte and its people. I told her to shut up and sing.

She'd brought along a little decorated Hottie drum for accompaniment. Are you sitting down, Hansie? This is what she offered.

Slowly, slowly over the little stones,
The rain falls wonderfully in little drops;
It's there where the sun and the moon go down –
Bookie, you must go home.

She sang that twice in a wavering shoestring voice, crouched on the floor flapping at the drum with her fingertips.

I held my hand over my mouth so she couldn't see me grinning. "Is that it?" I asked, coughing heavily.

"You like it, Commander?"

"The ends of the lines don't rhyme," I observed.

"They're not meant to rhyme, Commander," she said with a sugary little smile. "It's art."

"Art?" I spluttered.

"And it's also got a social message," she finished off.

"I tell you what, Beulah," I said, not wanting to hurt her feelings. "I think that you've got the right idea with your little song. You're definitely going along the right track. But I think we'd rather have something that at least rhymes and which white people would be proud to sing."

She started to protest but at a nod from me, Cheese threw her out.

"Well," I said after he'd closed the door, "that's another one of your fatuous ideas that's come to nothing. If we really need a National Anthem then let's ask them to find a professional in Holland who can write one properly."

"Would you like to hear the next submission, Commander?" he asked.

"How many more are there?"

"This is the last one."

I sighed. "All right, but that's all."

I'm so pleased I made the decision. Cheese opened the door and I heard the crack of a horsewhip. Into the office scuttled four of the Madagascar slaves neatly shackled together. One by one they fell to the floor and kissed my feet and then stood back. At a nod from their Slavemaster, George Hitler, they burst into harmonious song, their great white eyes rolling meaningfully in their happy coal-black visages.

Now, I'm no music critic, but I know what I like. They rattled their chains to a devastating light samba beat and you couldn't stop your foot tapping. The moment I heard the song I knew we'd got a winner. In the last verse I just managed to stop myself joining in. Now these are what I call good lyrics.

January, February, March, April,
May, June, July.
January, February, March, April,
May, June, July.
August, September, October,
November, December.

August, September, October,
November, December.

Hai!

January, February, March, April,
May, June, July.

Simple, to the point and everyone knows the words already. Cheese says it sounds too much like the calendar but I told him that's exactly the charm of the thing. I saw George Hitler walking across the parade ground later that day. I beckoned to him.

"I'm delighted with that song your slaves made up," I said warmly. "I hope you'll see to it that those four creatures are given some sort of appropriate compensation for their contribution?"

"It's already been done, Commander," he replied. "I've given instructions that they're to be given double rations of lice-ointment this weekend."

"Is that all?" I asked.

"Don't want to spoil them, Commander."

Remembering how much Beulah Cloete wanted to be involved in the new anthem, I called her in and told her to copy out the new song and then teach it to everyone in the settlement. She was still desperately trying to flog me her own ditty so I softened and said she could teach that one to the Hottie kitchen-staff.

All love to Hendrina and the little ones. I'm very touched to hear that you've named the new boy after me. His arrival must put the number of your offspring into double figures – in wedlock that is. I often wonder how many children I've really fathered. When I think back to those carefree Batavia days and those long months when Maria went off to Europe on her shopping trips. Those little virginal Javan teenagers were more than a man could resist. Oh well, I was younger then.

Yours in God

Van

My Dear Hansie

The *Vuildirk* sailed yesterday afternoon, taking with it a gentleman I wasn't sad to see the last of.

Luger Von Oyjk has spent the last six weeks here. He's a professional artist and he's being dispatched all over the world by Head Office to paint portraits of leading figures in the settlements. Apparently the Company has had a very profitable two or three years and so the Lords Seventeen have decided to adorn the walls in East India House with vast oil paintings of all the underpaid idiots like myself who were crazy enough to accept these assignments in uncivilised outposts.

In some ways Von Oyjk's visit occurred at just the right moment. I'd just had a couple of brand new outfits finished by the tailoring shop and my new blonde wig had arrived from Leiden. As I saw it, all I would have to do was dress up in my glad rags and perch motionless on a high stool for a few hours while Von Oyjk splashed my immortal visage down on canvas.

No such luck. Maria decided she wanted to get involved. We were half way through the first sitting when in she sidled and stood watching Von Oyjk work. I wondered how long she'd be able to keep her opinions to herself. As it turned out it was about three minutes.

She peered at the canvas. "You're getting his jaw all wrong," she said. "He hasn't got such a thick jaw, and his nose isn't nearly that straight."

Out of the corner of my eye I could see that Von Oyjk was not showing a lot of enthusiasm for this uncalled for criticism of his artistic abilities. He didn't say anything, just nodded and painted on with a grim little smile on his lips. Maria stood behind him squinting at his work.

"And I don't like the way you're doing his ears," she announced. "My husband's ears aren't that long droopy shape at all. You're making him look just like a turkey. And his wig looks like someone went and dumped a bowl of yellow macaroni on his head."

Von Oyjk was starting to bristle. "Commander?" he said softly.

But Maria was well into her stride. She turned her unwanted attentions to me. "Van," she said, "can't you smile just a little bit? You look so mournful."

"This is a mournful portrait, Maria," I hissed. "It's going to hang in Head Office. It's supposed to make people in Europe realise how much suffering and deprivation we colonists undergo out here in these lonely outposts. I can't sit here looking like a clown."

"I'm not asking you to plaster a big vacuous grin all over your face," she said. "I'm just saying you must try not to look as if you're about to have your piles drained."

I could see that Von Oyjk had stopped painting and was watching this little exchange with interest. I must say that for an artist he was showing a great deal of self-control. I'd heard these people are usually very temperamental. I was half expecting him to toss some sort of cultural fit.

Instead he gave Maria an ice-bound smile. "I think we may as well call it a day," he said. "Let's meet again same time tomorrow."

"You're stopping already!" Maria seemed outraged.

"I think I'll spend the rest of today painting some mountains," replied Von Oyjk.

"Well, all I can say is I hope you make a better job of those than that last painter, Schoutens, we had out here. He made them look far too pointy."

"I'll do my best," said Von Oyjk coldly. With a hot glare at me he swept out of the room.

I got hold of Cheese Blaauwtjopp later that afternoon and asked him to see to it that Maria was kept busy for the next week or so.

"What's Mrs van Riebeeck been interfering in now?" he enquired.

I explained at some length. He nodded and said he'd dredge up some urgent womanly task for her and which would keep her out of the way. It sort of worked except that, having got rid of Maria at the portrait sessions, Cheese felt his own advice might be useful. The very next day Von Oyjk and I were well into the next sitting when Cheese insinuated himself into the room. At first I thought he was going to be a help, but it didn't take long to see how wrong I was.

"That's quite wonderful, Mr Von Oyjk," he said, peering at the half-finished portrait. "You have captured our gracious Commander to perfection."

Von Oyjk preened himself at that. "Do you really think so?" he said with a giggle.

"Oh, yes," said Cheese warmly. "I particularly like the way you've put that no-nonsense intrepid-leader look in his eye. And you've got the wattled effect on the ears just right."

Von Oyjk preened himself even more at that. The two of them stood there chatting away like old friends. They discussed various parts of me and, I must say, Von Oyjk seemed to be lapping it all up.

"What's worrying me," said Cheese, "is the way you've got his left hand sort of plunging down into his cloak. It looks a bit suggestive having it in that position. You can't help wondering what he's feeling for down there."

They seemed to find that terribly funny.

"I've only got one other suggestion," said Cheese finally. "I think you should leave out that luminous purple rash on the throat."

"I thought it was rather realistic," was Von Oyjk's rejoinder. "Makes him look much more human."

Cheese scratched his chin. "I see your point. But then you are going to leave in those big yellow warts on the upper lip, aren't you?"

"Definitely."

At this point I called an end to the day's sitting. I took Cheese aside when Von Oyjk had packed up and left.

"You are worse than Maria," I growled.

"I thought I was being quite helpful," he said in a hurt tone.

"Go about your business, Cheese," I said, introducing a no-nonsense intrepid-leader look into my eye. "And see to it that no one at all interrupts these portrait sessions from now on. Including you."

He went off muttering and for the next few days Von Oyjk continued painting me without further aesthetic stimulation from family or staff. He refused point blank to let me see how the portrait was coming on, saying that this would compromise his artistic integrity. He said he only wanted me to see the portrait when it was finished. I grudgingly agreed. When he finished each session he draped a large oily cloth over the easel. It took all my willpower not to have a peep underneath it.

I wish I hadn't been so honest. Two days later I decided that I'd sneak up to the room we'd been using and take a look anyway. The portrait was gone. I sent for Von Oyjk.

"What have you done with it?" I demanded.

"Just taken it away for some final touches," he said lightly.

"What sort of final touches?"

"Nothing serious, Commander. Just putting those little extra highlights in your moustache and touching up the ruffle. Don't want you to have to sit around while I do all that minor stuff."

I could see he was lying but I didn't press the point in case he wasn't. Never get on the wrong side of the man painting your portrait for posterity, I always say.

Von Oyjk said he wanted to take a rest from gazing at me every day and was going to spend the next few days doing a group portrait of the senior Forte staff. He said that Head Office wanted something to show us all together looking like one big happy family with some nice landscape in the background.

What he didn't tell me was that his idea of a nice landscape included a couple of Hottentots. I said that was all right but that he mustn't paint them as sharp as he painted the white people. They should be sort of kept in the background and sort of misty.

"And try not to make their bottoms look too big," I added. "They don't like that sort of thing in Amsterdam."

I had to put my foot down when it came to who was going to be in the group portrait. I finally elected that Cheese could be there and also our Chief Flogger, Godjong Cloete. Hendryk Boom should be included since gardening was supposed to be our prime concern, and a representative from the military staff in Sergeant Klapmuts. Naturally I would be prominent in the group.

Instead of sitting in a cool room in the Forte, I now had to dress up in full regalia and stand for hours on a sand dune in the blazing sun with the others. What made it worse was that the two Hotties were up wind.

Maria got her bloomers in a real stitch when she heard that none of the women were going to be included in the group portrait. She went on whinging for hours, saying that it was typical of the male staff wanting to burgle all the historical glory for themselves.

"The womenfolk have also contributed to the success of this settlement," she whined. "Why can't we have our portraits painted, too?"

The only way I could calm her down was to ask Von Oyjk if he couldn't see his way clear to doing a quick painting of Maria while he waited for the *Vuildirk* to arrive and take him further on his travels. I said I didn't mind adding a little something to make it worth his while. It turned out to be quite a hefty little something but at that stage I'd have paid anything for peace. In the last few days before he left he whipped up a most passable head and shoulders of the goodly lady and which she's now hung over the bed.

I never did get to see my own portrait. There was always some excuse and only as I watched the *Vuildirk* disappear over the horizon did I realise that I should have insisted. Cheese told me that I shouldn't worry as he'd seen it and he thought that it was a truly noble representation.

"You'd be very proud of it, Commander," he said. "And he got your ears just right."

All for now. We've got a little expedition going up North to pick up some cattle from some Namas. I like to go along to keep an eye on the bartering. We're short of beads this year.

All love to Hennie.

Yours in God

Van

My Dear Hansie

I thought I knew what was meant by the term 'ungrateful'. But it took the attitudes and actions of certain of my colleagues to show me the true and dark meaning of the word. The Hottentot will steal you blind and live off your Christian charity for years on end and you'll never be in the slightest danger of hearing him say, 'Thank you, Master'. The Savage will sneak into the Forte at night and make off with your prize pigs without so much as a 'Thank you, my Baas'. These things you expect. What you don't expect is for a Dutchman to behave like that. You'd hope he'd have at least just a few manners.

No such luck!

At the beginning of this year we granted land and help to a group of the Forte staff, making them Free Burghers. As you know, nine of them had been granted this dispensation at my suggestion and had started up little farms around a river called the Amstel, near Rondebosch. The idea was that they could grow fresh fruit and veggies for the ships. It was my own little way of saying thank you to them, giving them a little stake in the country they'd helped to civilise. How did they respond to this act of Christian forbearance?

I'll tell you. Before you could say 'victuals' they had started a price war. They were trading with the ships at prices we couldn't possibly match from the Forte gardens. We have enormous overheads what with the staff to pay and all the maintenance necessary. Suddenly there they were, skulking around the jetty with great barrow-loads of produce and goats and sheep and the like.

I didn't quite know how to go about spiking their little game. Then we received a surprise visit from one Commissioner Ryner van Wyjq, sent here by Head Office to see whether there was anything he could 'rectify'.

Now I knew the Commissioner in Batavia where he was known as 'Snake-Shit' van Wyjq, and I have to tell you that he's a self-opinionated ballbag, forever sticking his long Flemish nose into the affairs of others. He's nasty and he's rude. He can't stand criticism even when, like mine, it's only constructive. He's vain and he's always been known to feather his own nest long before anyone else's. He seemed like the ideal man for the task.

In van Wyjq, Cheese Blaauwtjopp recognised a soul mate, someone nearly as devious as himself. They took one look at each other and you could see that they were going to hit it off. Inside a week they had come up with a way of ensuring that the Burghers could no longer indulge in their shifty practices.

This is how their system works.

Let's say that one of our Free Burghers, Godjong Cloete, wants to plant a field of brinjals. Before he pushes the first seed into the ground there are certain procedures he has to follow. First of all he has to make application in writing to what Cheese and van Wyjq have called the Brinjal Control Board. He sends them a letter asking permission to plant brinjals. He must also carefully write out the same letter nine more times and send these copies to various other people like Hendryk Boom, Chief Gardener at the Forte; to myself; to Head Office and, of course, to the Brinjal Control Board itself. The reason behind this is that all of the recipients of these copies of the letter are not only kept informed as to what Godjong Cloete is planning to do with brinjals this year, but also so that we can then make sure that not too many other Burghers have also decided to plant brinjals. With each of the ten letters that he sends out, Godjong Cloete has to enclose three guilders so that we all get something in return for the valuable advice the Brinjal Control Board intends giving him in the future.

Once we've all received our copies of Godjong Cloete's letter, we then immediately send each other letters to confirm that we've all received them. This takes only three months or so, though if the winds from Holland are a bit unfavourable, the letters to and from Head Office can take longer.

Once all the letters have been received and digested, the BCB members write long letters to each other, making suggestions about whether Godjong Cloete is using his wisdom in choosing to plant brinjals this year. These letters are then all eventually considered and all the officials of the Brinjal Control Board then get together for a piss-up which is called a Board Meeting.

The next step is that the Chairman of the BCB writes back to Godjong Cloete to tell him that his original letters are receiving urgent attention. In this letter he usually asks for further information so that a measured and wise decision can be taken. Godjong answers this letter with ten more, which are duly considered by the Board but only after the proper payment of thirty more guilders has been received.

Now things start getting exciting. Assuming that the Brinjal Control Board approves Godjong Cloete's application, the Chairman writes back to Godjong Cloete and encloses a DEIC 12/A Application Form for BCB-approved brinjal seeds. Godjong is advised in the strongest of terms that it will be illegal for him to use his own seeds on pain of flogging. He is also advised that his application for brinjal seeds will not be considered unless it is accompanied by the appropriate advance payment of another seventy guilders.

Duly Godjong Cloete's brinjal seed application is given consideration. Copies of the minutes of the latest Board Meeting are sent hither and fro and within three months the matter is finalised. Godjong is then informed that the brinjal seeds have been ordered from BCB-recommended stockists in Leiden and that as soon as they get to the Cape he will be informed. He is also informed that a BCB inspection team will shortly be sent to his farm to make a report on the suitability of the field he has chosen in which to plant his brinjals. It is pointed out that the costs of this inspection will be to his account.

When the seeds arrive from Holland, the Brinjal Control Board sends Godjong Cloete another letter telling him that the seeds are here but that they have been put into bond pending his payment of the import duty of another forty-three guilders. When eventually the BCB receives this payment from Godjong Cloete, things start moving at a fine old pace.

Godjong plants the seeds and gets the brinjals under way. At that stage another letter is sent to him advising him that the Brinjal Control Board wishes to be notified when the brinjals are ready for harvesting so that they can dispatch another inspection team to ensure that the brinjals are of the required standard. In this letter he is reminded – again in the strongest of terms – that no sub-standard brinjals will be accepted by agents acting for and on behalf of the BCB for later dispersal and supply to the ships.

Finally the day arrives when Godjong Cloete has harvested those brinjals that the inspection team has deemed to be of the approved standard. These are delivered to the Brinjal Control

Board's warehouse to await sale to the ships. Naturally, while the brinjals are in the warehouse, Godjong is required to pay adequate storage charges.

Once the brinjals have been sold, these storage charges are subtracted from the amount received, plus appropriate BCB commission charges and minus whatever brinjals have gone rotten. Godjong Cloete is then informed by letter that whatever monies are now due to him have been applied in part settlement of his overdue bill.

You'd think that such a simple and practical system would work without a hitch.

Again, no such luck!

I don't know where it went wrong, but apparently applications got mixed up, or people didn't fill in forms correctly, or didn't pay their accounts on time, or letters got filed in the wrong places. All the applications had been made and all the right channels had been gone down, but somewhere the BCB had mixed them all up. What resulted was a nightmare.

Not only Godjong Cloete, but several of his fellow Free Burghers all pitched up at the BCB warehouse on the same day with enormous wagon-loads of brinjals. Cheese told me he didn't think there were that many brinjals in the whole world. They totalled some eight thousand bushels.

"Even if everyone south of the equator eats nothing but ratatouille for the next six months we'll never be able to get rid of them, Commander," he wailed.

"What are you going to do?"

"We had an emergency meeting of the BCB last night and it was decided there were only two possible solutions. We can either load up all the extra brinjals on longboats, take them out into the bay and dump them overboard, or we can put up the price."

"Put up the price?" I asked in amazement. "You've more brinjals than you know what to do with and you want to put up the price!"

"It's BCB policy, Commander. If we bring the price down then the ships will buy more brinjals than they need and the BCB won't be left with enough to dump in the bay. We'll end up looking stupid."

"Why do you have to dump then in the bay anyway?" I demanded. "Why don't you just give them to the Hotties? I've never seen a Hottie that doesn't look half starved. They'd be only too grateful for some free brinjals."

He gave me one of his wistful smiles. "We can't give the extra brinjals to the Hotties, Commander. We'll set a precedent. Next year they'll expect more free brinjals and we might be short of brinjals then."

"It sounds to me like you're not going to be short of brinjals until about the middle of the eighteenth century," I observed dryly.

"Don't make light of this, Commander. A brinjal surplus is a serious matter," he said as he left.

I must say that I'm pleased to notice that Cheese has done something about his appearance. Recently he's been wearing a rather smart set of clothes, what with his new Gordonian ruffle and his hand-made Leipzig dancing pumps and new moleskin breeches. He's bought himself a spanking new two-horsepower Cape Cart which he says is necessary to befit properly his status as Chairman of the Brinjal Control Board. In fact, come to think of it, the other members of the BCB are also looking very well turned out these days. I wonder where they're getting the money?

Enough for now. I hear the supper bell ringing. I wonder what Maria's got in store for me tonight?

All love to Hennie and the little ones.

Yours in God

Van

Dear Old Hansie

We're stuck with our first political prisoner. Apparently he's been in our dungeons since late 1653. I had gone down there with Cheese Blaauwtjopp to inspect a drain blockage and in the back cell I saw this naked black creature shackled to a wall. I asked Cheese why I hadn't been told about him.

"Who's that?" I asked.

"His name is Drake Leadman, Commander. He's a prisoner."

"I can see that," I snapped. "What's he in prison for?"

"No one's terribly sure. He got arrested shortly after we finished the Forte late in 1653. I seem to remember he arrived here one afternoon and got into an argument with the Duty Sergeant. He claimed that we Dutch had no right to build a Forte here as this wasn't our country – something ridiculous like that. Anyway, he made a lot of other inflammatory remarks about white men, so the Duty Sergeant had him beaten and then locked him up."

I peered at the Savage. He looked to be quite a good specimen but a little wasted in limb after all the years he'd been hanging on the wall. He glared back at me with cold fury and contempt in his eyes.

"How long's he been here?" I asked.

"Eight years next Tuesday."

"He's been locked up here for eight years?" I asked incredulously.

"I think they forgot about him, Commander."

"Well, he must be released. Tell two of the soldiers to take him back to the edge of the forest and let him go."

"Do you think that's wise, Commander?"

"Don't argue with me, Cheese. Do as you're told."

Which of course, he didn't. I asked him a day later whether he had obeyed my instruction. He said he hadn't as he wanted to give me more time to think about it.

"What do you mean, you haven't let him go?" I demanded. "I told you to."

"I know, Commander," he simpered. "But it's not as easy as that."

"Why?"

"Because the Savage refuses to be released."

"Are you telling me he's enjoyed being shackled to a wall for eight years in an icy cold damp dungeon with no one but passing rats for company?"

"I think he sees himself as a political martyr, Commander. He says that he prefers to stay in the icy cold damp dungeon because by so doing he is proving that, despite what they're always bleating about Christian compassion, white men are actually a lot of unremitting shitbags."

"Does he indeed?"

"Whatsmore, he says if he is released he will devote the rest of his life to informing the civilised world about what disgusting and heartless bastards the Dutch colonists really are."

"Anything else?" I enquired sweetly.

"No. But it makes it rather difficult for us to let him go."

"What are we going to do with him?" I wondered.

Cheese smiled. "It's quite easy, Commander. We'll let him hang on the wall for a few more months and then we'll let him have a totally unexpected tragic accident."

"An accident?"

"Oh, he can fall down the dungeon stairs or something. Or we'll persuade him to commit suicide. All it needs is a little imagination."

I would have let it go at that except the next week the Captain of the *Vuildirk* dropped in to see me while his crew were loading brinjals for the journey east.

"I hear you've got yourself a celebrity," he said.

"What?"

"This jimfish prisoner of yours, Drake someone or other. Everyone in Europe's talking about him. They say he's got you by the short and curlies."

I couldn't believe it. "Haven't you heard?" he went on. "The Lords Seventeen have been getting a lot of flak about him. A couple of months ago someone stood up in The Hague and said that the Dutch East India Company should tell its staff out in the Cape of Good Hope to stop behaving like Germans."

"It's that bad, is it?" I said.

"What are you going to do about him, Jan?"

"Cheese Blaauwtjopp says we should quietly knock him off. Say he slipped on some soap and fell down the stairs and then say that we're terribly distressed about it."

"Sounds like a perfectly good idea to me," said the Captain. "But be careful. Cover your tracks."

I thanked him and when he'd gone I sent for Cheese. "What I want to know is who the hell found out about this Savage and went squealing all over Europe about him?" I demanded.

Cheese explained his theory on the matter. Apparently some passing sailors got horribly drunk one night and were thrown into the dungeons to cool off. One of them got to talk to this Leadman fellow who fed him a most frightful set of lies about how badly the Dutch were behaving out here. Without bothering to check with us, this sailor sneaked off back to Europe and wrote a series of letters to The Hague members and to the Court too. They spoke to others and the letters got copied and handed around the coffee-houses and before you could blink, Drake Leadman had become a hero.

"Who was this sailor?" I asked.

"We don't know his name yet, Commander," said Cheese. He dropped his voice. "But I understand he was Jewish."

"Typical," I said.

That evening I spoke to Maria about the problem. As usual she was ready with the perfect answer. Two days later, when the *Vuildirk* was safely on her way, I sprang into action. The Savage prisoner was brought up from the dungeons late at night. I told the two soldiers to see that he was bound hand and foot and that a canvas bag was tied over his head so that he couldn't bite anyone. They threw him in a longboat and rowed him away.

I've mentioned this small island out in the middle of Table Bay. It's desolate and bleak and no one ever goes there except occasionally to collect penguin eggs. I've often used it to get rid of undesirables. I told the soldiers to drop the Savage off on the shore and leave him there.

I went down to the beach and watched the longboat disappear into the night and then came back up here and wrote a report to Head Office saying that we woke up one morning to find that the Savage had escaped and that we haven't heard from him since.

Cheese rushed into the office the next morning.

"Commander, I've just heard what you did with Drake Leadman," he cried. "And I want to say your response was exactly what one would expect from a two-faced, underhand, callous and uncompromising colonial monster. Congratulations."

"Thank you, Cheese."

He was bubbling with enthusiasm. "I'll go so far as to say," he added, "that what you have done with this objectionable Savage will set an example all future Dutchmen will be proud to emulate."

So saying, he ran around the desk and hugged me warmly.

"It was really Maria's idea," I murmured.

"She's a wonderful woman, Commander."

So that's another little problem solved. I'm sure the Savage will find enough to eat on the island what with all the penguins and crabs and things, so I don't feel at all bad about leaving him there. He'll be a lot happier.

But we've learnt a lesson from this experience.

On a lighter note. I've been quite worried recently about finding something for the staff to do with their spare time. Now that we've got the basic building work done and the garden going well, we get these weekends where everyone seems to sit around at a loose end.

As it says in the Bible: the Devil makes much mischief for idle hands to do.

So I got a few of the fellows together and told them that they must try to encourage staff members to get out into the sun more often and not lie around in their hammocks when they are off duty letting their heads brim with sinful thoughts.

As usual Jackson Hoppelfoortj, Chief Prefect of the Brick Kiln, was full of useless ideas.

"Perhaps we could get a few of the chaps interested in card games?" he suggested.

"Are you mad?" I said. "Card games were invented and put on earth by Satan himself. With card games you get gambling and drinking and all manner of low activities. You'll have plenty of time for card games when you're dead and in hell."

"Just trying to help," he muttered sourly.

"Then try to at least come up with a Christian idea," I replied quickly.

"What about that game they all play in Batavia?" said our Goat Inspector, Breyten Greenlipp brightly. "I heard from some sailors that the Dutchmen over there have great fun throwing these old wagon-spokes at a stick in the ground."

"I've played that game," I said. "And I want to tell you it has got to be the most ball-crushing bore ever invented. It requires very little talent and no one understands the scoring. There's always too much arguing and it's also just another excuse to get together and drink heavily."

"Fishing," said our Slavemaster, George Hitler. "What about some fishing competitions?"

"Good idea," I said. "But not on Sundays, you understand. Sunday is the Lord's Sabbath and I'm not having people traipsing around in short trousers and draped with hooks and bait when they could be wearing out their knees giving thanks instead."

"I know," said Jackson Hoppelfoortj suddenly. "Why don't we have some Hottie hunts? What you do is you get hold of a fast young Hottie, take him out on the sand dunes, strip him naked and give him a thirty second start."

"And then?" I enquired.

"Well, about twenty of you run after him with horsewhips and sabres."

I could see there might be quite a lot of fun in his idea, especially if we could work in some sort of scoring system or offer a prize for first blood drawn, or something to give it an extra bit of spice.

"We'll give that one some thought," I told him. "But we might get complaints from the Hotties if we start doing this over weekends as well."

It was Naas Hoennervokker who came up with the most exciting idea. He's the Forte Swineherd and he's learnt to keep to himself. He'd been sitting quietly while we discussed things. Suddenly he piped up and told us that he'd seen a game played by some of the Bushmen up in Namaland. He said it's a traditional sport with them, but it seems to have distinct possibilities for white men.

"What they do," he explained, "is blow up this ostrich bladder until it's quite hard. Because the ostrich hasn't got too much space between its legs the bladder is sort of oval so when they kick it in the air you never know which way it's going to bounce when it comes down again."

"Go on," I said, trying not to smile too obviously.

"There are two teams of about fifteen Bushmen each. They draw two lines in the dust, about twenty roods apart, and the idea of the game is that the one side tries to carry the ostrich bladder over the other team's line while the other team tries to stop this happening."

"And what happens if they succeed?" asked Jackson Hoppelfoortj.

"They get points. Then they kick the bladder up in the air and all start again."

"Is that it?" I asked.

"That's the basic idea. But a lot else happens while each team is trying to get to the other team's line. There are all sorts of complicated rules like they aren't allowed to throw the ostrich bladder forwards and it musn't bounce before it goes out over the side lines. And every now and then they drop the bladder on the ground and everyone in both teams falls on top of it and tries to maim each other."

"I see."

"So there are lots of opportunities for kicking each other in the teeth and twisting necks backwards and gnawing each other's knackers and so on. The Bushmen don't believe it's been a good match unless at least three of them get killed," he finished triumphantly.

"If you ask me it sounds like a game for real arseholes," I observed. "I'm sorry, Naas, but I can't see any self-respecting Dutchman wanting to play a crude game like that. In the first place it obviously requires no intelligence and in the second it doesn't sound nearly dignified enough."

We dispersed without any other ideas being put forward. In the end I'm going to have to settle for the staff spending their spare time reading improving books. The trouble is only about two per cent of them can read.

Give Hendrina a big juicy kiss for me.

Yours in God

Van

My Dear Old Hansie

What does the word 'massage' mean to you?

I can tell you it's taken on a completely new meaning out here in the Cape of Good Hope. It all started when Head Office gave permission for ale-houses to be set up by some of the Free Burghers. These places were meant to be genial hostelries, their purpose to provide an evening of companionship and warmth, not only to the locals, but to passing sailors and merchants. These men, long distant from the comforts of home, wife and family, needed somewhere where they could drop in to share a glass of home-brewed beer and a merry joke or two with others like themselves.

They were not meant to be sinks of iniquity where any passing merchantman could indulge the sort of depraved fantasies that he and his filthy-minded shipmates had dreamt up on the dog-watch as they sailed along the Tropic of Capricorn.

It was that little scumbag Hendryjk Blem who first started the rot. He runs an ale-house about two Dutch miles from the Forte which he calls The Rub and Goffel. On the surface it all looked quite decent and Christian to me. But then I heard he'd got hold of some dissolute Hottie women and started offering what he called 'Exotic Relaxation Services' and 'Oriental Body Rubs' to his customers.

Just in case, I asked Cheese Blaauwtjopp to go and check out whether there was anything about Blem's operation I needed be worried about. He reported back a couple of days later.

"You can relax, Commander," he announced. "It's all quite wholesome and above board."

"You're lying," I replied coldly. "You can't fool me. I can see it in your face and I can see it in the way your left eyelid is twitching."

He looked as though I'd struck him. "Lying, Commander?" he protested. "Me?"

"Yes, you," I snapped. "How much has Hendryjk Blem paid you to hurry back here with this bucket of whitewash?"

"Well, since you put it that way, Commander," he faltered, "there are a couple of little things which I suggested could be cleaned up. But Mr Blem has agreed to do that of his own accord."

"Such as?"

I could see I had him on the hop as he waffled away, as devious as always. Eventually I squeezed it all out of him. It turned out that what was going on at The Rub and Goffel was even worse than I had feared. Apparently there isn't a sexual deviation or carnal delight invented which isn't available at Blem's degenerate establishment. It sounded just like Haarlem Moon, Madam Zzaj's joint up in the Hook, but with a lot of extras.

"But his prices are most reasonable," Cheese added.

I thought about this for a moment and then came to a difficult decision.

"It's quite clear to me that, as distasteful as these tasks can be, I would not be acting in a responsible fashion if I did not go and have a look for myself," I said.

"Will you be going alone, Commander?"

"When you're out on a mission to investigate moral decay at its source you should try not to involve innocent people."

"So you won't be taking Mrs van Riebeeck?"

"No."

I dropped in to The Rub and Goffel a few nights later, taking the precaution of disguising myself with large spectacles and a ginger wig. What I saw would have made the case-hardened Quartermaster blush.

The public rooms in the establishment aren't all that bad. Blem has employed our local dance-band, The Hottie Seven, on a contract. They play quiet polkas and jigs and the occasional slow allemande so that the younger folk can do a little smooching. There's nothing wrong with that. But I made a note to instruct Blem that having the ale dished out by young Savage womenfolk who have their upper parts uncovered is asking for trouble. I know that no Godfearing Dutchman would ever think of laying a lecherous hand on one of these indigenes, but why put temptation in their way? Why surround them with slender fifteen-year-olds with their firm perfectly formed breasts that glow so adorably in the candlelight, each one tipped with the soft roseate thrustings of upward-turned nipples?

At about eleven o'clock there was a long drum roll and Hendryjk Blem himself leapt onto the small stage in front of the band. I'd heard that he fancies himself as a good joke-teller, but I had no idea how good he really is. For a good twenty minutes he had everyone rolling around and bellowing with laughter as he told some wonderful stories and did what he called his 'impressions' of various officials at the Forte. I made a note to instruct him to cut down a bit on the below-decks kind of language he was using, but otherwise I have to admit that I laughed as much as the next man until he did what he called his 'Impression of a well-known Dutch East India Company Commander trying to find the outside privy on a moonless night'.

After that I had to dispatch about five extra ales to calm myself down – just as well because what followed confirmed my worst suspicions.

First they blew out all the candles in the place except those around the stage. Then a couple of sturdy men manhandled a great bed into the pool of soft light. Very softly the dance-band started to play a saraband in a minor key. A pair of stridently beautiful young Hottie women entered and began a strange and fascinating dance. They were dressed in transparent veils and carried tiny fans. At first they danced slowly, whirling the veils around in the air, but all the time, by deft manipulation of the fans, cleverly hiding their privates from public gaze. Gradually the rhythm of the band grew more intense as they writhed and murmured to each other, pretending to argue and at last falling onto the bed and starting to roll around, tearing and plucking at each others' veils. Suddenly from the darkness the lithe young figure of a man sprang into the light, his loins wrapped in a tiny cloth and his whole muscular body gleaming.

The two women cried out in fright as he leapt upon them, ripping away their veils. At this point I realised that I could no longer hold my peace. I leapt to my feet.

"Stop this immediately," I cried. "This is nothing other than the devil's work!"

I would have said more except the vast boatswain sitting next to me pulled me sharply back down into my seat and boxed me around the ear. I realised that he was just being sensible. There was no point in making a scene. I could always call Hendryjk Blem to my office later and remonstrate with him on a man to man basis.

I won't tell you in precise terms what I saw take place on that stage. There are some things a Christian should not try to describe. After the dance was over they lit all the candles again and I took note of the fact that many of the men present were being led into back rooms by the tasty little Savage waitresses. I thought I'd better have a look to see what was going on there, but another vast boatswain blocked my way. No matter how I protested he wouldn't let me past.

"Have to wait your turn like everyone else, won't you," he growled.

I started to protest but he took hold of my arm in an iron grip and led me gently out into the night. I couldn't afford to give away who I actually was so I had to suffer the heavy kick he gave me to help me on my way.

The next day I sent for Cheese.

"I made a discreet visit to The Rub and Goffel last night," I informed him. "And I have to tell you that I'm considering closing the place down and seeing that Hendryjk Blem gets a few hundred lashes for his trouble."

"Oh dear, Commander," he replied. "That would be a pity."

"What do you mean, a pity?" I seethed.

"Well, it's just that I don't think you should make any rash decisions, Commander," he supplicated. "I think you should pay a few more visits before you take any action. Don't rush into a decision you may regret in the passage of time."

I stared at him in amazement. "I don't care what you ..."

He raised his hand. "Besides which Mr Blem tells me he is changing the cabaret as from next week," he went on smoothly. "They've managed to get hold of this incredibly beautiful young woman from the East who's been working her passage to Europe by giving these really special solo entertainments at the outposts along the way." He paused and leaned close to me. "I hear she's Javanese."

"Javanese?" I croaked.

"Javanese, Commander," he smiled. "Surely you remember what those Javanese girls were like, from your days in Batavia?"

"That of course could put a completely different complexion on the matter," I admitted. "What disturbed me most last night was seeing sexually provocative behaviour where Hottentots were involved. I can't be seen to countenance that."

"Of course not, Commander," he said. "Whatsmore, Mrs van Riebeeck would be so grateful to you for your sacrifice. I know that she would be delighted to learn how your sense of duty had forced you to go and witness all that licentious behaviour without telling her about it.

"If by mistake she was ever to hear about it, that is," he added with a nasty edge to his voice.

"And the Javanese are very ... very ... you know ..." I murmured.

"Cultural?" he said softly.

That of course made me realise that I shouldn't be too hasty in making any decisions about The Rub and Goffel. I realised that it would be most insensitive of me to try to interfere with the cultural life of the settlement. After all, we get so few diversions out here. I told Cheese I'd think about it and sent him on his way. Next week I'll sneak in and see what the new show looks like and delay my decision until then.

No other news of any importance except we caught that little bugger Hottentot Harry. He'd escaped off Robben Island and was making off to the hinterland with a bundle of our best sheep and cattle. I don't know what to do with him. Flogging has no effect. There isn't a prison that can contain him. I'm afraid it's going to be a triple keelhaul this time.

Give my love to Hennie and the lighties.

Yours in God

Van

The Forte de Goede Hoop
8th May 1662

My Dear Hansie

Well, here goes. If the wind settles in we're off to Batavia tonight. We were expecting to go on the *Vuildirk* which would have been a far safer prospect for a long voyage. Instead we now face four months at sea on the *Mars*, shitting ourselves every rood of the way. Its Captain, one Galliard Botha, is a highly trained incompetent. I heard that the last time he tried going East he missed India!

I'm going to be sorry to leave this place. Despite everything that went wrong I don't think the last ten years has been a complete waste of time. Cheese Blaauwtjopp thinks otherwise.

"Another ten years from now, Commander," he said, "and they won't even remember we've been here. They'll talk about 'that chap they had in the Cape of Good Hope, Van Someone-or-other.'"

"What about all the journals and diaries we've kept so care-fully?" I said, feeling quite hurt.

"They'll be filed away in Head Office and forgotten."

I could see he was as depressed as I was. But then so many of Cheese's own plans have not worked out the way he wanted them to. For a start he needn't have bothered with his plan for a new simplified form of the Dutch language. It just never got airborne. Out here Dutch is showing signs of decay all on its own. It didn't need any help from us.

And then he spent nearly two years working on what he called the Tribes Register, the method he'd worked out for not only getting the Savages and Hotties in their place, but for keeping them there forever. He drew up a totally unique system whereby the indigenes were to be categorised according to the exact shade of their skins. It was a bit complicated as systems go, but it had a lot of merit.

Well, it got sent off to Head Office for approval. Did he get a note of thanks for all his work? Of course not. Instead, by return ship, Cheese received a curt note from some Secretary saying that in the opinion of the Lords Seventeen his Tribes Register was unnecessary. The tribes would keep to themselves all on their own. They had never mingled in the past and they never would. Moreover, the Secretary added, the white people would never interbreed with the Savages on any noticeable scale.

I wish they would. Perhaps a little Savage and Hottie blood would do us Dutchmen a power of good. Make us better able to deal with the climate. The Dutchman likes his rain and his wind and his icy cold. This place is far too hot and dry.

My own feelings are that we will never survive in this country. I'm not saying we don't have the staying power. But, being what we are, the most refined people in Europe, we will never be able to become dishonest enough. You have to learn to lie and steal and cheat to flourish here. It's a way of life.

Hottentot Harry said to me once, "Baas Jan, we just can't seem to teach you how to do it. There's such a lot of fun in swindling. Especially when you are busy crooking your own regime. That's the best of all."

Well, be that as it may, there are plenty of other reasons why we won't end up as permanent overlords of this place. Perhaps most important of these is that we simply can't breed quickly enough. I mean, the average Dutchman is quite happy to call it a day when the number of his offspring gets into double figures. But the Savage has no idea of population control. He just goes on and on and on. He's not satisfied with just one child every nine or ten months like us. The black man takes several wives, each one younger than the last – lucky sods. I heard of one Chief up north who, when he died, had no less than 148 children. It will be the downfall of us all. You can't negotiate when you're out-numbered twenty to one.

Oh well, time to close off. I see the flag is drooping and that means the wind is about to back. It'll be four months back to Batavia and then another eight after that for my next letter to get to you from there. So it'll be a year before you hear from me again. I'll scribble on the boat trip. There's nothing else to do.

Cheese is coming down to wave goodbye. I shall miss him and the intellectual stimulation he gives me. We had a lot of laughs too. He's going back to the Fatherland to take an early retirement.

Maria sends her love to you all, as I do. Have a prayer for us and ask that great Dutchman in the Sky to make sure Galliard Botha doesn't steer us into a whale.

Yours in God

Van